Essays on
German History
1862-1939

Edited by Gilbert Pleuger

Sempringham *publishing*, Bedford

Acknowledgements

The Editor acknowledges, with gratitude, the permission of the contributors to republish in this volume articles which first appeared in *History Review* or *new perspective.*

Sempringham publishing, Bedford, acknowledges, with gratitude, the consent of Gordon Marsden and History Today Ltd, 20 Old Compton Street, London W1V 5PE, who acquired *History Review* in 1992, to republish in Chapters 1, 2, 3, 6 and 7 articles from that journal.

Illustration acknowledgements

Mansell Collection p. 13; Hulton Getty Picture Collection pp. 21, 55, 65; Mary Evans Picture Library pp. 26 and 34.

ISBN 0 9515764 2 9

First published 1996

Sempringham Books, PO Box 248, Bedford MK41 0ZU

Copyright © History Today Ltd and Sempringham publishing (new perspective)

Chapter 1 Bismarck: The 'Iron Chancellor?' by Bruce Waller © History Review 1991, Chapter 2 Kaiser Wilhelm II and German History by Richard J. Evans © History Review 1991, Chapter 3 The Origins of the First World War by Volker Berghahn © History Review 1988, Chapter 6 The Determinants of German Foreign Policy 1933-9 by William Carr © History Review 1988 and Chapter 7 Did Hitler Want Total War? by Richard Overy © History Review 1989.

Chapter 4 From Weimar to Hitler: the Rise and Fall of the First German Democracy by E.J. Feuchtwanger © new perspective 1995, Chapter 5 The Rise of Nazism by Conan Fischer © new perspective 1996 and Chapter 8 The Hossbach Memorandum by William Simpson © new perspective 1996.

Cover portraits from top, clockwise: Bismarck in 1890, Kaiser Wilhelm II, Hitler and Stresemann. Cover portraits and text line drawings: Stephen Odom Designed and set by Sempringham publishing services, Bedford Printed by Redwood Books, Trowbridge, Wiltshire

Contents

Chronological overview

1862   Bismarck appointed Minister-President of Prussia
1864   Prussia and Austria at war with Denmark
1866   Prussia and Piedmont (Italy) at war with Austria
1866   North German Confederation created
1870-1 Prussia and other German states at war with France
1871   German (second) Empire declared at Versailles
1871   Bismarck created the imperial constitution
1878   Anti-socialist laws
1879   Tariffs for agricultural and manufactured imports introduced
1888   Accession of Kaiser Wilhelm II
1890   Wilhelm II engineered Bismarck's resignation
1890   Anti-Socialist laws not renewed
1898   Navy Law
1898   Beginning of Anglo-German alliance negotiations; later failed
1905   First Moroccan Crisis
1907   Triple Entente formed (France, Britain and Russia)
1912   Social Democrats became the largest Reichstag party
1912   Berlin War Council meeting
1914   28 June   Assassination of Franz Ferdinand in Sarajevo
1914   23 July   Austrian ultimatum to Serbia
1914   31 July   Russian mobilisation
1914   1 Aug.   German declaration of war on Russia
1914   3 Aug.   German declaration of war on France
1914   4 Aug.   British declaration of war on Germany
1916   German High Command gain *de facto* political power
1917   Social Democratic party split
1918   Mutiny by sailors at Kiel, revolt in Berlin. Kaiser abdicated
1919   Jan.   Spartacist rising defeated by *Freikorps*
1919   28 June   Treaty of Versailles signed by Germany
1919   Friedrich Ebert elected President of the Weimar republic
1920   Kapp putsch defeated
1923   Ruhr occupation by France and Belgium
1923   Out-of-control inflation
1923   NSDAP Munich 'Beer Hall' putsch defeated
1925   Hindenburg succeeded Ebert as President of the republic
1925   Locarno treaty signed
1926   Germany joined the League of Nations
1929   Wall Street crash
1930   NSDAP the second largest party in the Reichstag
1933   Hitler appointed Chancellor
1933   Reichstag fire. Enabling Law passed
1934   Night of the Long Knives
1936   Remilitarisation of the Rhineland
1936   Four Year Plan introduced
1938   *Anschluss* with Austria. Sudetenland crisis
1939   1 Sept.   German invasion of Poland
1939   3 Sept.   British and French declaration of war on Germany

1 Bismarck: The 'Iron Chancellor'?

Summary: Bismarck is portrayed as an accomplished political performer. His policies were not inflexible but, grounded on a sure grasp of Prussian state and conservative interest, were adapted in response to a realistic assessment of the needs of the State, the nature of the statesmen of the day and the circumstances of the situations as they evolved from 1850 through to 1890.

I T WAS 6 FEBRUARY 1888. The place was the old imperial parliament in Berlin. The new building was not completed until 1894. From the early hours of sunlight the atmosphere was charged with electricity. A dense throng surrounded the building. The public galleries were filled as rarely before; even the diplomatic boxes were all occupied. Prince William, soon to become Kaiser William II, was in attendance. By 1.00 pm two-thirds of the deputies had elected to skip breakfast and find their seats. Shouts of welcome from the press of artisans and clerks outside were audible in the chamber and heralded the arrival of Prince Bismarck, imperial chancellor. The tall, 72-year-old figure clad in cuirassier uniform entered from the back; the house rose until he had found his place. When the sitting opened, he took the floor and addressed the chamber in his somewhat incongru- ously high and thin voice which his admirers called soft, but his opponents more realistically labelled squeaky. His son, the secretary of state in the foreign office, stood a few paces to the rear and periodically handed the speaker a glass containing an effervescent but not altogether colourless liquid. The two-hour speech ranged widely over German foreign policy, especially relations with Russia. It was conciliatory and peaceful, but it would have been untypical had it contained no barb. Germany, he said, would not start a war, but, if compelled, she would defend herself with 'teutonic fury'.

Phrases in History

As if to reward those who had patiently followed his homilies on statecraft and peace he uttered a ringing peroration: 'We Germans fear God and nought else in the world.' It did not matter that the speech had been sensible though tedious, nor that it was an exercise in night-time whistling.

The country was very much on edge because the Russians were in one of their periodic warlike moods, moving troops on to the frontier and attacking the Germans in the press. Many felt that spring would bring war against France as well as Russia. Some looked forward to this; most did not. The speech was meant to warn, but also to assuage the Russians; in addition, it was meant to calm German public opinion. Politicians took note of this. But the public heard only the defiant 'We Germans fear God and nought else'. These few words made this the most famous speech in Bismarck's entire career. The tumultuous applause echoed through the house and accompanied him as he walked the short way back to the foreign ministry, making his way through adoring crowds, protected all along by his vigilant son. Those in the street had no idea what he had said but, gathering that it must have been momentous, expressed approval. I think we have a lesson here in mass psychology.

Putting an original gloss on the passage that Germans feared only God, Tsar Alexander III sent Bismarck a 'big barrel of caviar'. We do not know whether he ate it all at once but, considering Bismarck's gargantuan appetite, he probably did and so proved that he feared only God. The speech served its purpose as a move in foreign affairs: Alexander was apparently appreciative. It also united Germany as had nothing previously. Within days trinkets were sold all over Germany with the proud phrase inscribed on them.

Bismarck had been in office for just over 25 years. He was to remain in office for just over 25 months. Never before had he honed a phrase so appealing to the national spirit. Never again would he succeed so brilliantly.

The glorious phrase was not a flamboyant challenge to the world, but rather an artful disguise for a peaceful and unadventurous policy. Perhaps the iron chancellor was going rusty. Let's glance at something he said within days of taking office as prime minister of Prussia. It was in a budget committee meeting on 30 September 1862. Bismarck tried to persuade the few MPs present that if parliament could not agree on a budget, the government could carry on without one. The committee members objected. On this occasion the prime minister's hands shook; his speech was even more unsteady than usual. As on the public occasion 25 years later he wanted concessions for the army. But he was not terribly belligerent. He sought to underline his desire for accommodation by using temptation: his adversaries on the budget committee were liberals who wanted to extend parliament's control over government. They were also nationalists. Bismarck therefore hinted that the winter of their discontent might well precede a blissful summer. He said: 'Prussia must build and preserve her strength … Her borders under the treaties of Vienna are unfavourable for the health of the State. The great questions of the day will not be settled by

Bismarck: The 'Iron Chancellor'?

Bismarck in 1850 (left) and 1890 (right)

speeches and majority decisions - that was the great mistake of 1848 and 1849 - but by iron and blood.' Note the correct phrasing: 'iron and blood'. In the spirit of ham-acting he emphasised the real purpose of these remarks by extracting from his cigar case, a tiny olive branch which he had retained as souvenir of a prolonged flirtation with a Russian princess. He was sentimental enough to have such a memento, but not so sentimental as to avoid using it!

Bismarck's talks on 30 September 1862 with his adversaries on the budget committee did not win them over. The initial newspaper reports were also neither full nor unfriendly. It was only later that the crisp phrase - 'iron and blood' - was regarded as the distillation of his politics and led to the epithet 'iron chancellor'. So this archetypal martial phrase does not, if seen in context, reveal the mind of a cavalryman in full gallop with lance lowered.

Perhaps Bismarck may have been rusty in 1888. But his behaviour in 1862 does not appear to be very ferrous at all. We can interpret these two wonderfully masterful Bismarck quotes - the two best known ones - as examples of steely determination. We can see now that another interpretation is also possible: the iron chancellor was perhaps more of an alloy - closer to brass than to iron.

Well, perhaps we have not gone back far enough in his career. It is possible, but improbable, that he was already oxidising in 1862, and if we look back another dozen years, we can find a Bismarck of burnished iron.

On 3 December 1850 he spoke in the Prussian parliament. Like the other two occasions, this was a time of tension. In early 1888 there was danger of war with Russia; in 1850 it was with Austria. On the earlier occasion Bismarck, typically, spoke for a good long while. Amongst other things he uttered the following words which have been quoted a thousand times over: 'The only sound foundation of a great state ... is state egoism and not romanticism ... it is unworthy of a great state to fight for something in which it has no interest.' Now, these are words, if not of iron, then at least of flint. The words in praise of 'state egoism' are not a description of reality, but a prescription of what ought to be - unabashed 'me firstism'. In 1850 Bismarck was only an MP, but we surely have the 'iron MP', or do we? Let us cast an eye on the accompanying circumstances. After the collapse of the revolution of 1848 the Prussian king, Frederick William IV, tried to unite much of Germany under his lead. In November 1850 Austria stopped this at a meeting in the Moravian town of Olmütz. Prussian historians have ever since called this the 'humiliation of Olmütz'. Many Prussians were furious at the royal climb-down and wanted to fight. In those days it would have been very much more arduous than 16 years later. Bismarck was not quite sure whether to approve or disapprove of the Olmütz agreement, but was charged with defending it in parliament. So the speech from which the phrase was lifted and enshrined egoism was not warlike at all; just the reverse. And the man who defended his government's statesmanlike but uncourageous capitulation was not very sure what he was doing.

Realistic Politics

We have now three famous appearances - two in front of parliament and one before a parliamentary committee; we have three well-known statements on politics spanning a period of 38 years - virtually the whole of Bismarck's political career. All three look bellicose but, seen in context, they were defensive - not very peaceful, surely, but also not very warlike.

The 'iron MP', the 'iron prime minister' and the 'iron chancellor' were not wrought from pure iron. If we regard Bismarck as a forceful, determined and blinkered brute, we are wrong. A good number of other clichés about him are wrong too: he was not, for instance, the implacable foe of Liberals and the inveterate friend of aristocrats. What was he then? If we want to stick a label on him, then let us call him a *realist*. This realism was the handmaiden of the State which he saw as an instrument of power. 'Isms' meant little to him unless they could strengthen the State with which he of course identified himself. This was the point where his realism broke down. He regarded opponents as his, and the State's, enemies, and so persecuted them with irrational fury. They, his enemies, were to be found in all groups of society - Conservatives, Liberals, Democrats, Socialists, Protestants, Catholics, etc. The degree to which he personalised domestic politics was quite unrealistic and caused much ill-feeling. He was more hard-headed in foreign politics because he could see that other state leaders could legitimately oppose him in the interests of their own states. But his famous acid rivalry with the Russian chancellor, Gorchakov, shows that animosities were at play in his foreign policy as well as in his home politics.

Personalised Politics

So Bismarck's state and power-orientated realism was marred by a weakness for personal vendettas. His vendettas were not indiscriminate; he had good political reasons for them. It was a question of exaggeration: where he should have been firm, he was harsh.

When we think of the 'iron chancellor', we see in our mind's eye a man with iron will, a tough, inflexible man, impervious to outside influence. Our three quotations from 1850, 1862 and 1888 could well stem from such a man, but if we consider the circumstances in which each was made, not one of these qualities seems to fit; we see no unbending will but self-doubt and a desire for compromise and conciliation; the toughness appears as posturing; inflexibility becomes reasonable determination; we can see in each of the three situations that Bismarck was very open to outside influence.

When we think of the 'iron chancellor', we think also of power politics, that is, the use of force where persuasion would suffice. The situations in which Bismarck made each of our apparently power political statements show that he preferred persuasion to force. If we think of the 'iron chancellor' we miss the essence of the man. If we think of a realist, we get much closer.

I would now like first of all to deal with Bismarck's approach to politics, then the evolutionary nature of his policy before the founding of the empire in 1871, finally there will be a few words about foreign policy after 1871.

Development of His Domestic Creed

First his approach to politics - not his policy as such, but how he behaved as a politician: When Otto von Bismarck entered politics in 1847 he was a man from the sticks. His horizon reached as far as a covey of partridges rising from the coppice. He was a country-gentleman, gun in hand and dog at heel. He was a reactionary; his politics were guided by a conservative ideal. But it was conservatism with a vengeance. The revolution of 1848 taught the lesson that ideals alone are worth little. They have to be bonded to the practical interests of people. They can receive tangible reinforcement only by making compromises with reality. Bismarck was quick to realise this, and so he dumped his conservative convictions in favour of a line oriented almost solely on state aggrandisement. One can understand this

Development of His Domestic Creed　　　　　　　**5**

reaction at the time, since most European regimes collapsed in 1848 and it was natural to think that they needed strengthening. The quotation taken from December 1850 concerning state egoism illustrates this magnificently. So Bismarck swiftly turned from the furrow of conservatism to the battlefield of state egoism. This was a remarkable and vast change. From 1850 until he died in 1898 a whiff of gunpowder accompanied him. His approach did not undergo much further change, but it changed in a critical way: in the course of the fifties he realised that a policy based merely on state aggrandisement would not work in the nineteenth century when one needed the voluntary co-operation not merely of a coterie of pampered aristocrats but of hundreds of thousands of men. He talked and wrote unceasingly, trying to win converts, but to no avail until the end of the Crimean War when he began to realise that his fairly bloody-minded policy needed softening. He had to adopt some of the national and liberal platform of his contemporaries. By the end of the fifties - well before he assumed high office in 1862 - he knew that old Prussian ways could be preserved only by strengthening the State; and the State could be strengthened only by sacrificing much to the national and liberal movements. He knew that if he tried to keep everything, he might lose everything. His chances of keeping half, by sacrificing the other half, were excellent. Since he was almost the only Prussian who thought on these lines, he was also well poised to run the State himself.

Students make the mistake of labelling Bismarck a 'typical Junker'. He wasn't; and the 'typical Junkers' hated him. Bismarck guided Prussia and Germany through a period of hectic transformation - very much more rapid than the simultaneous changes occurring in this country. The Junkers abominated almost all of these changes.

What does this mean about Bismarck's approach to politics? He began as a conservative, a reactionary idealist; by late 1850 he had become almost a power politician; by 1860 he had become a realist who was not afraid of power but was guided partly by national and liberal idealism and partly, of course, by traditional conservative values. His approach did not alter much after this.

Foreign Policy: Austria, France and Dominance

Let us turn now to the evolutionary character of his policy. Bismarck was first and foremost a diplomatist. His formative years - the fifties - were devoted exclusively to foreign policy and diplomacy. The sixties were taken up largely by foreign affairs. His subsequent political views were critically influenced by these experiences. The fact that he ran the German empire from the Prussian foreign office is not without significance.

The key to Bismarck's foreign policy and indirectly through that to his domestic policy is his attitude to Austria. The envoys of the German states discussed joint affairs in Frankfurt at the diet of the German Confederation. Bismarck went there as Prussian representative in 1851. His instructions were to work in harmony with Austria. A superficial interpretation of his speech in December 1850 pointed to him as the ideal man for this. Apparently, no one understood that his emphasis on state egoism as superior to any of the political 'isms' would prove a big impediment. The Austrians were determined to run the show in Frankfurt. Bismarck tried to co-operate on the basis of equality, but they did not want that, so he very soon decided that Germany should be divided between them - Prussia taking the north and Austria the south. This would not have united Germany, and so it ran against the grain of national-liberal sentiment. In addition, Austria was not interested. So, by 1859 at the latest, Bismarck abandoned this line and aimed for Prussian dominance in Germany. This was an ambitious goal, but working for it enabled him to obtain the support of the national-liberals. In a way it was easier to follow a more ambitious policy than the less ambitious one!

Power and the Barrel of the Gun

From the mid-fifties he grew increasingly certain that decisions would come through gunfire. French and Piedmontese success in 1859 encouraged him to think that a call to arms could produce useful results. The war showed also that Austrian determination left much to be desired. There was only one snag. Prussia had mobilised during the war, fearing that, once in action, the French army would cross the Rhine. This mobilisation went badly. The army made many rectifiable errors, and was lucky enough to have Moltke at the general staff to locate them and seek correction.

It is fairly certain that Bismarck aimed at gaining ascendancy in Germany when he took office. He tried to reach his goal without using the army, but never really thought this would work. He felt that the army reform was important, for without it a military clash with Austria would fail. When he was made prime minister in September 1862 the king, William I, was on the verge of abandoning his struggle with parliament over the reform. A partly reformed army might still have beaten the Austrian forces, but in war luck cannot be commanded, and so it was better to have overwhelming superiority.

A prolonged contest between Austria and Prussia had filled the middle of the previous century. Ever since, Prussian and Austrian statesmen had eyed one another uneasily. The two powers were in a state of agitated equilibrium. Austria had the advantage in the early nineteenth century; afterwards the scales tipped towards Prussia. An armed contest between these secular rivals had an air of inevitability, and was preferable to continued friction between the two camps. The later battle between France, Prussia and her allies was by no means as sensible or even likely.

French ascendancy and security had traditionally lain in a divided Germany. Neither her ascendancy nor her security was threatened greatly by the results of the Austro-Prussian War in 1866. Germany was still sufficiently divided so as to be of no real threat to the French. But France did have less freedom than previously to pursue an ambitious line. Politically aware Frenchmen felt this keenly and so sought to whittle away Prussia's gains. We are fairly certain that Bismarck believed that the gains made through the war with Austria would take many years to consolidate. But he could see also that the jittery French might unwittingly accelerate the process and even, by posing an external threat, precipitate final unification.

The Match for the Day

Within a year or two after 1866 Bismarck realised that the French were spoiling for a fight. He could have avoided it by making a series of minor concessions; but peace would have remained precarious. He reasoned that conciliation offered small advantage and possibly greater disadvantage. A courageous line, however, could bring impressive gain. The likelihood of disaster could not be completely discounted, but it was relatively small. He did not work single-mindedly for war, but since he saw little point in avoiding it, he steered with a few tacks here and there in the direction of military show-down. It was as if Napoleon and Bismarck were in telepathic communion because each thought that war was, on balance, more desirable than peace. The war of 1866 could not easily have been avoided and did serve a useful purpose. The Franco-Prussian war could have been avoided although it also served a useful purpose: it led to almost complete German unification; it also brought home to the Austrians that some settlement with the new empire had to be reached; Bismarck too came round to this view, and in October 1879 Austria and Germany formed the Dual Alliance, the first of the pre-First World War alliances. Thus Bismarck finally attained in 1879 that for which he was commissioned in 1851 when he went to Frankfurt. One wonders whether there could have been a shorter route to this goal.

Bismarck had no overall plan from the start; his policy changed quite radically over the years. At many stages he would have accepted compromise with opponents, but after he entered government he felt that war would more likely benefit Prussia than his enemies. He could not be sure, and so was fairly cautious.

Post 1871: The Politics of a Pessimist

We turn now to Bismarck's approach to foreign policy after the founding of the empire in Versailles on 18 January 1871. The sixties were a period of movement and expansion. All this was hostage to fortune. Bismarck was

8

no adventurer, and once the empire had been established, be became a good deal more cautious. Apart from the overseas colonial surge in the mid-eighties there was no further expansion. He sought to guard what he had achieved, using methods he had learned in diplomacy. He was a pessimist. He did not believe that his accomplishments would last forever, nor did he anticipate a roseate future. He strove not to change men - a pointless exercise - but rather to direct them so that their bad habits could serve the general good. He tried to create what Medlicott has called a 'balance of tension' at home and abroad. He gave this idea classic formulation in his well-known Kissingen dictation in June 1877: what he wanted was a political constellation in which all the powers, except France, needed Germany and were kept from an opposing coalition through their relations with one another. This was the essence of his foreign policy: a dynamic balance; the other powers were neither to be on excellent nor on awful terms with one another, but to remain suspicious and therefore in need of German backing. Bismarck sought not ascendancy, but merely to be in the midst of things, surrounded by quarrelsome powers looking to him for guidance. But he was temperamentally unsuited for this role which demanded unrelenting patience and goodwill (which he did not have) in addition to profound political understanding (which he did have).

Dynamic Balance

Similar tactics were used at home. If his foreign policy was not as successful as many historians believe, his domestic policy was not as unsuccessful. The constitution for the North German Confederation of 1867 was adopted by the empire. It was very largely his work. It was a skilful balancing act and accurately reflects Bismarck's approach to politics. Its federalism balanced traditional provincialism against new nationalism; conservative ways were heavily off-set by liberal innovations. We must not think that the irascible man himself was balanced - he was not; the *Kulturkampf* and the persecution of socialists show this clearly enough. But, apart from this, he did create a rough-and-ready balance in Germany, a dynamic balance of seething discontent rather than of honeyed sweetness (a will-o'-the-wisp anyhow). When he reluctantly retired in 1890 the emperor, aristocrats, the middle classes and workers had all profited up to a point from his handling of affairs. Each felt cheated - as did other groups: Liberals tell us that the chancellor was beastly to them; aristocrats had similar complaints. The truth is that Bismarck went about his job in a realistic manner. He was also a pessimist and a cynic; he used mankind's bad habits to consolidate state power and his own. He was a good deal more sophisticated than the facile phrase 'iron chancellor' indicates.

Questions to consider

- What distinguished Bismarck from the Junker interest?

- What evidence is there from Bismarck's policies and actions of self doubt and a willingness to compromise?

- How far were Bismarck's achievements founded on his astute appreciation on Man's nature and in foreign relations, the capacities of neighbouring states?

- If a key characteristic of Bismarck the politician was a willingness to change, from the perspective of German history, 1850-1950, what was his greatest mistake?

Further reading: Introductory texts; G. Kent, *Bismarck and His Times*, Illinois, 1978; B. Waller, *Bismarck*, Oxford, 1985; D. Williamson, *Bismarck and Germany, 1862-90*. Further texts: W.N. Medlicott, *Bismarck and Modern Germany*, London, 1965. This is the best brief treatment. Page 160 contains the reference to a 'balance of tensions'. Many of his seminal ideas are elaborated in: L. Gall, *Bismarck the White Revolutionary*, 2 vols, London, 1986. Gall provides the most profound full biography. See also: O. Pflanze, *Bismarck and the Development of Modern Germany*, 3 vols, Princeton, NJ, 1990. Pflanze's biography is magisterial and very full and the newest study. W.L. Langer, *European Alliances and Alignments*, New York, 1931, is a classic statement maximising Bismarck's mastery. It is a widely used university lecturer's crib. W.E. Mosse, *The European Powers and the German Question, 1848-1871*, Cambridge, 1958, minimises Bismarck's achievement. It has an admirable concluding chapter. William Carr, *The Origins of the German Wars of Unification*, London, 1991, is the newest handy survey.

Dr Bruce Waller is the author of **Bismarck at the Crossroads, 1974, and Bismarck, Historical Association Studies, 1985.**

2 Kaiser Wilhelm II and German History

Summary: Professor Richard J. Evans charts how German historians viewed Wilhelm II's reign as a Golden Age when
compared with the instability and damage sustained by Germany
in the decades after 1914. Röhl's thesis of a Wilhelmine government system is viewed with caution and contrasted with the
importance given to social and political interests after 1870 which
German historians have increasingly stressed since the mid
1960s. Further, Professor Evans questions the significance of the
continuation of authoritarianism in society and politics. While the
new wealthy bourgeoisie chose not to be associated with the
conservative establishment and the Social Democratic party and
gave primacy to economic rather than to political interests, it was
a complex intermesh of interactive forces between change and
conservatism which forged Germany's history both before and
after the First World War. From this dominant characteristic,
which Wilhelm II embodied in the paradoxes of his character,
there was no necessary or inevitable development towards the
Third Reich.

LOOKING BACK over the violent and catastrophic history of Hitler's
'Third Reich', German historians of the older generation tended to see
the Germany of pre-1914 days as a haven of peace and tranquillity in
comparison to what followed. Before the First World War, they believed,
law and order reigned on Germany's streets, economic growth and
industrial prosperity created peace and contentment among Germany's
population, naval and military strength guaranteed the inviolability of
Germany's borders, and scientific, educational and cultural achievements
made Germany's name respected in the civilised world. But, after more
than 40 years of such stability, the guns of August 1914 ushered in a period
of upheaval and disaster. Encircled by hostile and jealous foreign powers,
Germany was forced into a war on two fronts that could not be won. The
Treaty of Versailles imposed vindictive and humiliating restrictions on her
international status. Armed revolutionary bands roamed the streets from
1918 onwards, while counter-revolutionary hit-squads eliminated a whole
series of leading political figures. Hyperinflation destroyed savings and

made money valueless. The Depression threw millions out of their jobs. Communists and Nazis clashed with increasing frequency and ferocity. Hitler's advent to power, though it promised a return to order, led before long to a renewed bout of violence and war that ended in the horrors of the death camps and the destruction and division of Germany. In little more than three decades after the end of the long Bismarckian and Wilhelmine peace, Germany was occupied and the boundaries of the Bismarckian Reich had been drastically curtailed. No wonder, then, that many German historians who had lived through these traumatic events looked back with nostalgia to the days of imperial tranquillity before 1914.

Different Perspectives

Yet, to others, the contrast appeared deceptive. If Germany had been encircled by foreign powers in 1914, was that not to some extent her own fault? Surely, it was reasoned, the seeds for the disasters of the interwar years must have been sown long before 1914. Perhaps the unification of Germany achieved by Bismarck had not been without its own potential dangers, from the Machiavellian amorality of Bismarckian *Realpolitik* to the popular glorification of the armed might demonstrated in the victorious wars of 1866 and 1870. But at least Bismarck had known when to stop. Indeed, he had spent his last two decades in office attempting to secure Germany's position in Europe through an elaborate structure of diplomatic treaties and alliances. It was not until Kaiser Wilhelm II began his 'personal rule' after having engineered Bismarck's resignation in 1890 that things began to go seriously wrong. Impetuous, headstrong and determined to be 'his own Chancellor', Wilhelm proceeded to upset the precarious inter-national balance achieved by Bismarck, by a string of ill-judged actions and remarks, ranging from his telegram of congratulations to President Kruger of the South African Republic on the repulse of the Jameson Raid in 1895 to the notorious interview with the *Daily Telegraph* in 1908, in which he claimed to have been the author of the military strategy by which Lord Roberts had won the Boer War. The Kaiser, it has been said, approached every question with an open mouth; more often than not, too, he put his foot in it.

On a different level from such gaffes was the Kaiser's rage against the Serbs in 1914, which led him to scribble violently bellicose comments in the margins of the dispatches he received during the final crisis of July and early August. And his unbridled enthusiasm for the construction of a large German battle fleet was more serious still. Not only did he shower the Navy leadership with carefully-drafted designs, in his own hand, of new battle cruisers, he did his utmost also to appoint men in the relevant posts who would be sympathetic to his naval passion. A big German battle fleet could really be directed against only one other power - and that was

Britain; and of all the factors which contributed towards the growing hostility between Britain and Germany from the turn of the century onwards, there can be little doubt that the construction of the German High Seas Fleet under the guidance of Admiral Tirpitz weighed heaviest in the balance.

A Wilhelmine System: Fact or Fantasy?

The thesis of the Kaiser's 'personal rule' has recently been taken up, extended and considerably refined by Professor John Röhl, in a series of painstaking archival researches that have brought to light a great deal of new - or previously suppressed - material about Wilhelm II's extraordinary personality and actions. This material, he argues, demonstrates that 'personal rule' was really more a system of government centred on the Imperial Court, rather than just a series of individual actions by the Kaiser. Moreover, Röhl suggests that Wilhelm was not merely tactless and outspoken, but so mentally unbalanced that he can be regarded to all intents and purposes as having been mentally deranged. Certainly there

Kaiser Wilhelm II in 1895

A Wilhelmine System: Fact or Fantasy?   **13**

was a streak of insanity in the Hohenzollern family. As recently as the mid-nineteenth century, King Friedrich Wilhelm IV of Prussia had been certified mentally unfit to govern, and his functions had been handed over to a regent, his brother the future German Emperor Wilhelm I. A number of doctors testified to the pathological streak in the personal make-up of Wilhelm II, and stories of the Kaiser's eccentric and disturbed character were legion, though often suppressed from public view during his lifetime.

A full and balanced assessment of this interpretation must await the completion of Röhl's biography of the Kaiser, currently in progress. In the meantime one should sound a note of caution. The diagnosis of insanity, or even of a manic-depressive syndrome such as Röhl has suggested the Kaiser was suffering from, is fraught with difficulty, especially if it is retrospective and the subject is no longer alive to be questioned or examined. The categories and definitions used by the leading psychiatrists of the late nineteenth century, many of whom (including the great Sigmund Freud himself) commented critically on the Kaiser's personality, cannot be taken as 'scientific' in the light of present-day knowledge. Indeed, modern historians of medicine and psychiatry warn strongly against regarding medical theories and diagnoses, especially in the area of personality disorders, as objective assessments unmediated by the social, cultural and political values and norms of the society in which they are made. Moreover, a social historian would have to point out that many aspects of Wilhelm II's behaviour which may seem bizarre today, such as his frequently rude and boorish demeanour, his crude and sometimes sadistic practical jokes, his love of dressing up, his preference for much of the time for all-male company, and so on, were widely shared among the international high aristocracy of the era.

Court ceremonial, elaborate orders of precedence, militarism and public schooligansim in high society, and personally irresponsible beha-viour on the part of the monarchs and princes, were by no means confined to Imperial Germany. They were present just as much in Britain, where the unsavoury and scandal-ridden character and entourage of the Prince of Wales (later King Edward VII) were similar objects of gossip and speculation among those in the know. It is arguable that to regard the German court as a mechanism of rule is to mistake appearances for realities, especially in view of the manifest failure of so many of the Kaiser's pet projects, from the 'Revolution Bill' and similar legislative initiatives of the 1890s onwards. When we look at the private opinions of his senior ministers and top civil servants, Wilhelm appears not as steering the ship of state towards a predetermined goal but as periodically intervening to blow it off course. As a consequence, they found themselves frequently obliged to embark on hastily contrived damage-limitation exercises. True to his restless and erratic character, the Kaiser spent much of his time travelling rather than in engaging in the business of government; and his histrionic outbursts, his grandiose statements and his bombastic rhetoric were widely recognised for the froth that they were.

Bismarck's Legacy: Prussian Conservative Interest Entrenched

Most historians writing in the last 25 years or so would probably agree that, while the Kaiser's defects of character and abuse of his undoubtedly wide-ranging powers are factors that no serious student of the age can afford to ignore, it was in the end not so much Wilhelm's 'personal rule' that propelled Germany towards the abyss of 1914, as a combination of wider and more impersonal forces. From the 1960s onwards, German historians began to view the Wilhelmine era with a much more critical eye than they had done before. They came increasingly to identify the sources of Germany's travails in the twentieth century not in the Kaiser's personality but in the whole social and political structure of the Empire created by Bismarck. They pointed out the fact that the Imperial constitution entrenched the domination of conservative Prussia over the more liberal states of the South and West; that while the parliament, the Reichstag, was elected by universal manhood suffrage, ministers were appointed by the monarch and could not be voted out of office; that crucial institutions such as the Army were effectively beyond the control of the legislature; and that in Prussia itself - the larger part of the Empire, with widespread autonomy to run its own internal affairs - elections were held on a restricted franchise skewed in favour of the well-off. There was, they believed, something profoundly wrong with a political system that remained so unresponsive to popular opinion that the party with the largest number of seats in the Reichstag shortly before the First World War - the Social Democratic party - was not only denied all access to power but was also effectively ostracised by the entire Establishment, and its members barred from most key institutions of state and society.

The Liberal and Social Democratic historians of the 1960s and 1970s concluded, therefore, that democracy and parliamentary rule never really arrived in the German Empire, despite all the trappings and appearances. Authoritarian police controls, including the persecution of Catholics during the *Kulturkampf* in the 1870s, the banning of the Social Democrats in the 1880s and their continued harassment thereafter, and the repression of national minorities such as the Poles, revealed, perpetuated and eventually deepened the weakness of liberal values such as toleration, freedom of speech, and popular sovereignty. The low priority given to democratic and human rights in German political culture, they argued, had its ultimate roots in the failure of the liberals to seize power in 1848. Had the Frankfurt Parliament succeeded in the Revolution of that year and united Germany under the auspices of liberal idealism, the future course of German history might have been very different indeed. But the unification of Germany was achieved not by votes and majority decisions, but, as Bismarck said, by blood and iron. Using revolutionary methods for conservative ends, Bismarck stole the liberals' thunder and forced them to accept national unity in a form which, not least by thwarting their original wish to include Austria, guaranteed the continued domination of the traditional Prussian élites - the landed aristocracy, the generals, the senior civil servants and the rest.

As time went on, so these historians argued, the challenge to this domination grew. Rapid industrialisation was transforming the face of Germany in the last decades of the nineteenth century and giving increasing weight to modern social classes such as the bourgeoisie and the proletariat. The response of the élites to this challenge was twofold. On the one hand, they tried to co-opt the upper middle class - especially the industrialists and higher professionals by offering them the opportunity to gain more wealth (for example, through state arms contracts for industrialists, or legal guarantees and support for professionals) and the means to win greater social prestige (for example, through the granting of titles or recruitment into the reserve officer corps). These tactics, it is argued, successfully won a large proportion of the middle classes over to a conservative, anti-democratic way of thinking. On the other hand, the élites tried to keep the threat of socialism at bay not just through police repression but also through bread and circuses, above all in the colonialism of the 'Scramble for Africa' in the 1880s and the imperialism of the scramble for a 'place in the sun' announced by Chancellor von Bülow's *Weltpolitik* from the end of the following decade onwards. This, it is argued, was the real structural imperative behind the course taken by Germany's foreign policy up to and including the declaration of war in 1914, which is regarded, above all, as a gamble by the German élites launched in a desperate attempt to divert the attention of the masses from the need for democracy and reform and win them over to a nationalistic endorsement of the *status quo*. All this, finally, goes a long way towards explaining why liberal and democratic values could not take root in Germany and why, therefore, so many millions of Germans repudiated the Weimar Republic in 1932-3, voting, a mere one-and-a-half decades after the abdication of the Kaiser, for the demagogic, militaristic and anti-democratic programme of Hitler and the Nazi party.

Thus, Germany had taken a different route to the modern world than that trodden by Western countries such as Britain. Industrialisation had generally been preceded by the political triumph of the middle classes over the aristocracy, as in France in 1789; but in Germany things were different. Here industrialisation took place under the auspices of an authoritarian political system that perpetuated the social and political subordination of the bourgeoisie. Only with the final defeat of Nazism in 1945 was the legacy of the failed 1848 Revolution taken up again; only then did the three central features of the 'modernisation process' - a booming industrial economy, a stable democratic polity, and an open, meritocratic society - come together at last in Germany. In these terms, German historians linked Wilhelm II's reign to the wider course of German history. But their interpretation, as we shall see, is just as open to criticism as its predecessors.

Germany was not Exceptional

There is a problem with the 'structural' view of modern German history. If we take our eyes away from the British example for a moment and look more broadly at the European scene, the evidence for the exceptional nature of Germany's development seems a good deal less strong. Countries such as France and Italy, for instance, underwent major episodes of authoritarian politics during the process of industrialisation. Indeed, the Second Empire in France and the Fascist era in Italy were both periods of outstandingly rapid industrial growth. Conversely, progress towards democratic politics could be steady and sustained in a basically agricultural nation such as Denmark. On the other hand, similar arguments about the persistence in power of a feudal or neo-feudal aristocracy as the basic cause of the breakdown of political consensus, the rise of extreme nationalism, the escalation of political antagonisms and the eventual triumph of brutal authoritarianism, have been advanced for other countries besides Germany, most notably for Spain. The American historian Arno J. Mayer has even gone so far as to argue that the 'old regime', dominated by the aristocracy, persisted everywhere in Europe, including Britain, right up to the First World War. Such a sweeping hypothesis is, in the end, perhaps not very persuasive; but what the implausibility of Mayer's argument ought to suggest, like any comparative perspective on the whole of Europe, is that there was in reality no single, fixed, 'normal' road from the politics of the pre-industrial world to the politics of advanced industrial societies. Each nation had to find its own way, and this was as true of Germany as of any other country.

Non-assimilation of Aristocratic Values

Recent work in the field of social history has begun to reveal that Wilhelm II's Germany was in some ways much more modern than many of its Liberal critics have supposed. Real evidence for the notion that the middle classes were backward-looking and 'feudalised' is hard to come by. The view that they scrambled for titles turns out, on closer inspection of the statistics for ennoblement, to be exaggerated. Few of the wealthiest industrialists and financiers of Imperial Germany acquired landed estates

Non-assimilation of Aristocratic Values   **17** or titles of nobility. In some places, such as Germany's second city and leading trading centre, Hamburg, pride in being bourgeois was so great that titles and orders were generally rejected when they were offered. Even the habit of duelling, in which bourgeois men indulged until well after the turn of the century, was intended to assert the equality of bourgeois honour with aristocratic honour. Industrialists in Germany have often been accused of adopting an 'aristocratic' lifestyle and of treating their workers like serfs; but few of them in fact bought or built castles, and most of them lived in comparative modesty. Much as it may have suited the propagandistic purposes of trade unionists, whose members were barred from working in firms like Krupp's, to have accused the bosses of antiquated attitudes towards labour relations, banning trade unions was, after all, very much in the interests of keeping up profits, and the weakness of collective bargaining structures in Imperial Germany was, above all, due to the opportunity given the employers by the large scale and close intermeshing of Germany's major business enterprises. In many ways, German society before the First World War was characterised not by 'feudalisation' but by embourgeoisement - the spread and general triumph of middle-class rather than aristocratic values.

The Evolution of Junker Interests

Where the bourgeoisie was undoubtedly weak was on the political front, with the lack of parliamentary power and the fragmentation of the party system. Yet here, too, it is much too simple to describe Wilhelmine Germany as having been ruled by 'the Junkers'. In the 1870s, indeed, the Prussian aristocracy was deeply unhappy about the form taken by German unification. It continued to grumble well after the turn of the century at the way things were going. The Junkers could demonstrate their political muscle in getting import duties on corn raised in 1879 and 1902, but other interests lay behind these measures too, and the Junkers were in the end less than happy with what they got. Their ability to control and manipulate Reichstag and Prussian elections was rapidly undermined after the turn of the century. Their power over the army officer corps was steadily diminishing, and the new navy was dominated by officers from middle-class backgrounds. The Junkers themselves were becoming more modern. As their legal rights over the land and those who lived on it were steadily whittled away, the old patriarchal social relations that had survived the abolition of serfdom in East Elbian rural society earlier in the century were replaced by modern capitalist farming methods, in which cheap migrant labour was employed in increasing quantities and growing numbers of peasants were thrown off the land or left it for work in the towns. Modern farming methods were introduced, and the production of crops like sugar beet was complemented by diversification into modern rural industries like the refining of sugar or the distilling of rye or potato brandy.

The New Nationalism

The Junkers' power to manipulate popular politics now appears to have been substantially overestimated in the literature of the 1970s. There was, of course, aristocratic and even government involvement in the rise of new, aggressively nationalist movements such as the Navy League, or the Society for the Eastern Marches. But there was also an independent input into the new nationalism from below, from discontented lower-middle-class elements, led by professional demagogues drawn from a variety of sections of society. Before long, therefore, an organisation such as the Navy League was split by internal quarrels, as the radicals began to berate the government for not building the High Seas Fleet fast enough; while the pan-German League, on the eve of the war, was directing fierce criticisms against the Kaiser and his ministers for being weak-kneed and liberal, too tolerant of subversives within Germany and too conciliatory towards Germany's enemies abroad. Radical nationalism was not a creature of either the Junkers or the government; it had its own dynamic and by 1914 it was getting rapidly out of control. Apart from the radical, pan-German nationalism which some elements among the middle and lower-middle classes supported, there were other varieties of nationalism as well. Many liberals coupled the assertion of Germany's great-power interests with a desire for domestic social and political reform. When the leader of the National Liberal Party, Ernst Bassermann, was offered a ministry by Reich Chancellor von Bülow, he refused to accept unless some of his party colleagues were given ministries too, thus in effect creating a party government and therefore to some extent a parliamentary government. This was something Bülow felt unable to accept. Among the left-liberals, there was growing support for the doctrines of Friedrich Naumann, who preached a combination of imperialism and social reform in order to persuade the working class to abandon the idea of a socialist revolution. And it is important to note that despite their loss of support before the turn of the century, left-liberals remained the most popular party among the middle classes in Germany's towns and cities right up to the First World War.

The Social Democratic Party and the State

To many participants and observers, the most striking development in German politics up to 1914 was the seemingly unstoppable rise of the Social Democratic Party, until it had over a million members and more seats in the Reichstag than any other political grouping. Formed under the aegis of Marx and Engels, it was committed to a socialist revolution by its party programme, formulated at Erfurt in 1891. The party was unremittingly critical of the central institutions of the Wilhelmine Empire - the monarchy, the Church, the Army, the education system, the civil service and, above all, industry and business. The party leader August Bebel declared that the whole structure of Wilhelmine Germany was a gigantic system of exploitation of the poor by the rich and powerful. He urged his supporters to give 'not one man, not one penny' to 'this system'. The party's deputies in the Reichstag demonstratively refused to stand and cheer the Kaiser as the other deputies did at the beginning of each session, and at the Party Congress the members seriously considered the proposal to stage a mass general strike to bring the government down and force the capitalists to capitulate.

A Toothless Tiger

Such views were very frightening to the German middle classes. Scarcely less terrifying were the more immediate aims of the Social Democrats, which included the introduction of universal and equal adult suffrage at every level of the Empire's constitutional structure (including Prussia) and the establishment of full, democratic civil rights in every area. But in many ways by 1914 the Social Democrats' bark had outgrown their ability to bite. While working-class poverty and deprivation on the one hand, and police and official hostility on the other, combined to ensure that the party remained aloof from the existing political system, beneath the surface things had begun to change. A new generation of party leaders took over from Bebel, who had partially retired some time before his death in 1913. Many of them, such as Friedrich Ebert, were in practice prepared to compromise with the Wilhelmine state; to accept, for example, a constitutional monarchy instead of a socialist republic. They preferred to work for an improvement in living standards and an extension of civil rights in the present and put off plans for a revolution indefinitely. Working-class poverty was becoming less acute, and rank-and-file Social Democrats, who in any case mostly belonged to the upper levels of the proletariat, were beginning to feel that they had more to lose than their chains. The growing professional party bureaucracy was naturally even more susceptible to such feelings. Above all, the party and the trade union movement (the bulk of which was closely allied to the Social Democrats) became increasingly committed to a policy of remaining within the law once Bismarck's ban was lifted in 1890. The discipline and orderliness of the German Social Democrats were legendary far beyond the borders of Germany itself. It was, after all, Lenin who once remarked that the German socialists would never be able to stage a successful revolution because they would not dare to storm the main railway stations without buying platform tickets first.

Assimilation Consummated

Finally, when faced with the evidence of the political duplicity, the brutal repression, and the anti-Semitic pogroms that accompanied the reassertion of authority by Tsar Nicholas II after the failure of the 1905 Revolution in Russia, the Social Democrats concluded that whatever the imperfections of the Wilhelmine political system, it was infinitely preferable to the arbitrary and despotic violence of Tsarist autocracy. This was the fundamental reason why, contrary to their declared policy of opposing war as a capitalist enterprise in which the workers would be no more than mere cannon-fodder, they agreed to vote for war credits in August 1914, as Reich Chancellor Bethmann Hollweg successfully persuaded them that they were defending their country against Russian aggression.

The Force of the New and Survival 'of the Old'

All this suggests, in the end, that the future in 1914 was a lot more open than many recent historians have suggested. Germany might have moved in any one of a number of different directions. The potential for liberalisation was as great as that for a slide into dictatorship. What tipped the balance, though still far from decisively, was the cataclysmic impact of the First World War. The war lasted far longer than anyone thought, and its effects were far more profound than anyone anticipated. It left a working class radicalised by years of hardship, shortages and, towards the end, hunger and starvation; a middle class divided by the effects of

Friedrich Ebert who later became the first President of the Weimar Republic

The Force of the New and Survival 'of the Old'   21

rampant inflation; a nationalism rendered bitter and resentful by the consequences of defeat. Popular pressure, the voice of the crowd in the streets, was what eventually forced the Kaiser to go and brought the Weimar Republic into being. The Social Democrats' leader Friedrich Ebert said, 'I hate revolution like sin'; but he went along with the masses because otherwise he feared he would be swept away in a German version of the Bolshevik revolution. There was in fact no German Lenin. The Social Democrats managed an orderly transition of power. But it was at a price. By allying with the Imperial army, administration and economic élite in order to do so, they had helped these institutions to survive into the new era of democracy, where they quickly began to attack the republic and work for a restoration of the monarchy or, increasingly, the creation of an ultra-nationalistic dictatorship.

Inevitability Challenged

Despite the severe problems which it confronted, however, the Weimar Republic was by no means as inevitably doomed from the outset as recent historians have suggested. Here, too, it is necessary to stress the openness of possible outcomes, even with the onset of the world economic depression at the end of the 1920s. What the Weimar Republic went through was in many ways a classic crisis of modernity, of rapid economic, social, political and cultural change, that profoundly dislocated and radicalised the political culture of the day. But this crisis had in fact already begun in the last years before the outbreak of the war. Wilhelm II's Germany was a society in transition. It presented a startling mixture of the old and the new: a hide-bound court and military aristocracy, a passion for hierarchy and order, a political regime with a strong element of authoritarianism, a large peasant sector whose attitudes and practices were far removed from those of modern capitalist farming, an artisan community, also numerically strong, that looked back nostalgically to the days of the guilds, before markets were free; but also an industrial economy that was the largest, most efficient and most productive in Europe, a parliamentary system whose elections attracted a percentage poll of over 80 per cent, an increasingly technocratic attitude to military and naval affairs, a turbulent cultural scene in which modernist novelists, playwrights, painters and musicians were causing growing controversy among the public, an emergent women's liberation movement that reflected as well as to some extent promoted the involvement of women in politics, the decline of the birth-rate and other modern developments in this area, a new mass media including not only popular newspapers but also the cinema, and a novel form of populist politics, led by demagogues and propagandists, of a kind that was to reach its logical conclusion after the war in the likes of Hitler and Goebbels.

Wilhelm II: the Embodiment of Paradox

What ultimately makes the figure of Kaiser Wilhelm II himself so fascinating is the fact that he expressed these paradoxes in his very person: on the one hand, an enthusiast for military and especially naval technology, for new inventions of all kinds, for industrial power, for the modern world; on the other, a believer in the divine right of monarchy, in the duty of his subjects to obey, in the destiny of the Hohenzollerns, in the recreation of the supposed glories of the past. The kind of historical mystification in which he indulged was to re-emerge in a more radical form in the pseudo-medieval mythology created by the Nazis. In the end, therefore, Wilhelm II was perhaps less important for what he was than for what he symbolised: the need for invented tradition to cushion the shock of the new, the failure of that tradition to overcome the deepening social and political antagonisms that the strains of rapid modernisation were creating.

Questions to consider

- How convincing is the thesis of a 'Wilhelmine system' and the arguments for a structuralist interpretation of the history of Wilhelm II's reign?

- How great was the threat posed by the Social Democratic party, its organisation, leadership and ideology, to the political system of Wilhelmine Germany?

- 'The locomotive of change in Wilhelm II's Germany was, as Marx predicted, economic change'. Do you agree with this assessment?

- How far can it be argued that the underlying tone of Weimar Germany and its collapse was set by Wilhelm II's reign, not by the post-1918 political, financial and economic crises?

Further reading: Hans-Ulrich Wehler, *The German Empire 1871-1918*, Leamington Spa, 1985; Gordon A. Craig, *Germany 1866-1945*, Oxford, 1978; John Röhl (ed.), *Kaiser Wilhelm II: New Interpretations*, Cambridge, 1979; David Blackbourn and Geoff Eley, *The Peculiarities of German History*, Oxford, 1984; Richard J. Evans, *Rethinking German History*, London, 1987; Richard J. Evans (ed.), *Society and Politics in Wilhelmine Germany*, London, 1978.

Richard J. Evans is Professor of History and Vice-Master at Birkbeck College, University of London. His books Death in Hamburg: Society and Politics in the Cholera Years *(Penguin, 1990) and* Rituals of Retribution: Capital Punishment in Germany 1600-1987 *(Oxford University Press, 1996).*

3 The Origins of the First World War

Summary: Despite the amount of work on the origins of the First World War, debate continues on the allocation of responsibility and the motives of the key personalities. Fischer's work has focused attention on Berlin and Vienna but the debate continues on whether the German declaration of war in 1914 was part of a long-term plan, with the intention to achieve international power-political aims or to resolve domestic tensions, or the result of a train of escalating events which began with the Serajevo assassination.

THIS ARTICLE on the origins of the First World War is not concerned with the broad background factors (imperialist rivalries, the arms race, nationalist public opinion) which one finds discussed in the textbook literature on this subject. Rather it tries to take stock of the recent debate on the immediate causes of the catastrophe that hit Europe in 1914 and, in a second part, to suggest a theme which you may wish to pursue in your essay or project work.

Thanks to the by now well-known Fischer Controversy of the 1960s, students of the pre-1914 period find themselves in a uniquely favourable position: there is today a rich monographic literature which covers the foreign and domestic policies of most of the major powers which became involved in the First World War. Better still, useful syntheses of this research are available in inexpensive paperback editions. In particular, the Macmillan series is virtually complete. The early volumes in this series on Britain and Germany have recently been complemented by studies on Russia, Italy and France.[1] The volume on Austria-Hungary, the only major country still missing, is currently being written by the American historian Samuel Williamson and should be published in due course. Finally, in 1984, James Joll published a most valuable paperback which tries to pull together the scholarship of the past 20 years and which culminates in an analysis of the 'mood of 1914' and the values of this period.[2] For it is by these values, Joll believes, that the actions of the 'men' of 1914 should be measured.

And yet, however rich the material and however comprehensive the work already done, it would be a mistake to assume that our factual knowledge and understanding of the pre-1914 period and its problems is now as advanced as it will ever be. On the contrary, there are territories still to be explored, and no doubt future historians will turn their attention to them. Nor would it be accurate to say that the *debate* on the origins of the First World War has come to an end. In fact, fundamental differences of opinion persist when it comes to allocating responsibilities for the 1914 catastrophe or to discussing the motives that guided those who pushed Europe over the brink. Let us therefore turn to these areas of disagreement before we begin to identify one of those big topics on which all too little is known to this day and which future historians are likely to turn their attention to.

Pointing the Finger: the Contribution of the Fischer Debate

As to the continuing debate on the origins of the First World War, it may be said that the Fischer Controversy has, if nothing else, clarified one central point: in searching for those responsible, we no longer have to go on a grand tour of Europe's capitals.[3] While not denying that it is worthwhile to study the moves of the British, French or Russian governments during the July Crisis, most of our time should in fact be spent examining the documents from the files which piled up in Berlin and

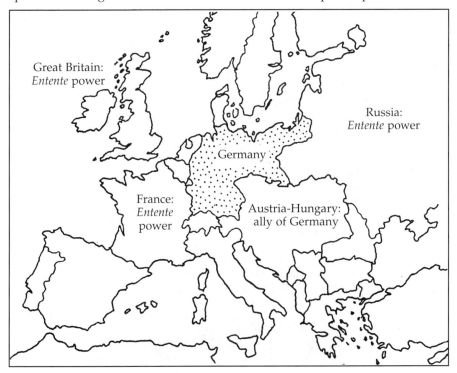

Germany and her neighbours in 1914

The Contribution of the Fischer Debate   **25**

Vienna. Of course it has been Fischer's argument from the start that this be done. But he is confirmed in this by the previously-mentioned studies in the Macmillan series. Only L.C.F. Turner has focused on Russia as the main culprit.[4] But it is not my impression that this view has been accepted by other experts in the field. A related point of Fischer's has also been accepted, namely that it was not *the* Germans or *the* Austrians who unleashed the First World War, but rather a clearly identifiable group of top decision-makers. To be sure, these men believed themselves to be under considerable outside pressure. They worried about the press and their country's international standing. Nevertheless, the small circle of people had sufficient power and room for manoeuvre to produce a result short of war. But instead of opting for this, they deliberately escalated the management of the July Crisis 1914 into a major war, even though they were in the best position to de-escalate it, if they had wanted to.

These conclusions, derived from the outcome of the Fischer Debate and the new documents recovered from the archives during the past 20 years, are not meant to imply that historians also agree on why the 'men of 1914' started a major war. On the one hand, there is Fischer who has essentially stuck to his guns. In his first book, he had argued that the German government was in an aggressive and expansionist mood and tried to implement by force territorial and power-political aims which had been developed in the years before 1914.[5] This, it seemed to Fischer, was the

Bethmann Hollweg

The Contribution of the Fischer Debate

only plausible explanation for why Reich Chancellor Theobold von Bethmann Hollweg had been able to draw up the (in)famous September Memorandum which, a few weeks after the outbreak of war, brought together wide-ranging demands for territorial annexations which had been submitted to him as soon as the fighting had begun. Fischer therefore sees the policy of the Dual Alliance and in particular that of the Kaiser and his advisers as guided by assertiveness and ruthless determination. Above all, he thinks, the Berlin government aimed for a major war from the start. The well-known 'blanc cheque', issued to Vienna on 5 July 1914 and assuring Austria-Hungary of full German support, was, at least according to Fischer, designed to achieve nothing less than the unleashing of a general conflict with the Triple Entente. There may have been some people in Berlin who held hopes that Britain would remain neutral. But a war against Russia and France was thenceforth being prepared.

The Significance of the Berlin War Council, December 1912

This argument concerning the expansiveness of Germany's calculations and ambitions at the beginning of the July Crisis 1914 was subsequently sharpened by Fischer when documents were discovered relating to a 'War Council', held in Berlin on 8 December 1912. The origins and consequences of this hastily convened meeting between the Kaiser and his top military advisers are being discussed in greater detail in Fritz Fischer's *War of Illusions*.[6] According to the records, Helmuth von Moltke, the Chief of the General Staff, used the occasion of the meeting with the Kaiser to press for an immediate war against France and Russia. Alfred von Tirpitz, the Navy Secretary, whose naval building programme had run into trouble, argued for postponing war by 18 months. It was only in the summer of 1914 that the widening of the Kiel Canal would be completed, enabling the Navy's largest and latest battleships to move quickly between the Baltic and the North Sea and thus facilitating a powerful concentration of the imperial fleet, built up since 1898. War, so Fischer continues, was accordingly postponed. Meanwhile, and on the Kaiser's orders, all measures were to be taken to rearm the country and to prepare the public for an impending major war. In particular, the Russian menace was to be built up.

Given that the Reich government did in fact introduce a massive Army Bill in 1913 and that the right-wing press stepped up its xenophobic propaganda, there is a good deal of plausibility in Fischer's hypothesis concerning the crucial importance of the War Council of December 1912. However, his critics have tended to play down its significance. They have pointed to the assessment of the conference by Georg Alexander von Müller, the Chief of the Naval Cabinet, on whose diary entry much of our knowledge of the meeting is based. He recorded that the results were 'pretty much nil'. The critics have also stressed that, given the Kaiser's erratic and volatile style of government, it is difficult to see how Berlin could have arrived at, and decided to pursue, a cold-blooded decision to go to war 18 months from December 1912 after the completion of the Kiel Canal. Most importantly, other historians have insisted that full account be taken of developments in 1913/14. Looking at the state of German domestic and foreign policy, they feel that the position of the Hohenzollern monarchy experienced a rapid deterioration in those 18 months. It was the impact of this deterioration upon the German leadership and the military in particular which nurtured thoughts of a preventive war against France and Russia - a conflict unleashed not from a sense of assertive recklessness with the aim of achieving world-power status by means of a victorious war, but from a feeling of deep gloom. The Prusso-German monarchy should strike before it was too late.

As regards Germany's foreign policy position, the mood is seen to be very clearly reflected in a memorandum which Foreign Secretary Gottlieb von Jagow wrote after a meeting with Moltke in May 1914:

> The prospects of the future seriously worried him. Russia will have completed her armaments in 2 to 3 years. The military superiority of our enemies would be so great then that he did not know how we might cope with them. Now we would still be more or less a match for them. In his view there was no alternative to waging a preventive war in order to defeat the enemy as long as we could still more or less pass the test. The Chief of the General Staff left it at my discretion to gear our policy to an early unleashing of a war.

The Political Situation in Germany

The domestic situation in Germany looked no more promising from the point of view of the Kaiser and his advisers.[7] The Social Democrats, whom they perceived to be dangerous revolutionaries, had risen to become the largest party in the German national Parliament in the 1912 elections. Bethmann Hollweg had had tremendous difficulties in getting the 1913 Finance Bill through the Reichstag which was supposed to raise sufficient revenue to pay for the 1913 rearmament programme. The so-called Zabern Affair, in which the Army and the monarch found themselves widely criticised because of their handling of clear violations of the law by officers in Alsace-Lorraine, was seen as a bad omen for the future stability of the monarchical system. Watching these developments with concern, some right-wingers apparently began to think of a swift victorious war as a means of getting rid of the 110 Social Democrats in the Reichstag. It seems that in this they took as their model Otto von Bismarck, who had held elections in Prussia following his victory over Austria in 1866, and, by exploiting the general patriotic euphoria, had routed the opposition in the Diet. No doubt a victory in 1914 would have done much to stabilise the increasingly precarious domestic position of the Hohenzollern monarchy.

Were German Plans after June 1914 Limited or Not?

Yet, even if the German military and certain Conservatives were, by the summer of 1914, thinking of a preventive strike, in the eyes of Fischer's critics this did not mean that Berlin immediately decided upon starting a major war when Archduke Ferdinand and his wife were assassinated by Serbian nationalists at Sarajevo on 28 June 1914. Rather the initial strategy was to encourage Austria-Hungary to achieve a limited success against Serbia in the Balkans and thereby to stop a further deterioration of the international position of the two Central Powers.[8] Only, so the argument continues, when this limited war strategy turned out to be founded on illusions and miscalculations, because Russia could not be kept out of an Austro-Serbian conflict, did the military appear on the scene to press for a major war. This argument is based on newly discovered documents, such as a memorandum by Tirpitz's deputy, Admiral Eduard von Capelle, who saw the Kaiser on 6 July, on the day after the 'blanc cheque' had been issued. According to this memorandum, Wilhelm II made the following points:

> His Majesty does not think it likely that Russia will come to Serbia's support, as the Tsar would not wish to aid those implicated in a regicide and as Russia was militarily and financially totally unprepared for war. The same applied to France, especially as far as her military preparedness was concerned. His Majesty did not mention Britain. But he had told Emperor Francis Joseph that he could rely on him. His Majesty believes that the situation will have been cleared up within a week due to Serbia's compliance. But he felt that one must also be prepared for a different result.

The diaries of Kurt Riezler, the Reich Chancellor's private secretary, rediscovered in the 1960s and finally published in 1972, seemed to confirm these limited calculations, that is, to achieve a diplomatic *fait accompli* through a humiliation of Serbia and thereby to stabilise the position of the Central Powers and of the ramshackle multinational Habsburg Empire in particular.[9] Unfortunately, the authenticity of the crucial passages in the Riezler diaries relating to July 1914 is now in serious doubt. What, according to the painstaking researches of the Berlin historian Bernd Sösemann, we have got is a later and most likely 'laundered' version of the original passages. This discovery, first published in 1983, came as a considerable shock to scholars who had trusted the 1972 edition of the diaries. More significantly, it was seized upon by Fischer. He argued, using evidence from the 1950s, that the original had apparently been destroyed, because it contained very compromising statements showing Berlin's determination to launch a major war from the start. However, since the protagonists of the 'limited war' calculation continue to uphold their case, the debate concerning both the deeper motives and the immediate strategy pursued by Berlin after the Sarajevo assassinations will no doubt continue. Interpreting the relevant documents, most of which have by now been published, from the perspective of Fischer and his critics is therefore still an intriguing task.

The People's Response to War Reconsidered

While this particular argument will no doubt be carried forward and be fought over among political historians, using ministerial files and diplomatic despatches, a new field of research and argument has recently been opened up which is likely to expand during the next few years. The discovery of this field is related to the rise of social history and the 'history from below'. With social historians in large numbers now studying the experience and mentalities of ordinary people through the ages, it was perhaps inevitable that they should also begin to study popular moods and reactions to the July Crisis and the outbreak of the First World War. Of course, there has always been an assumption that the so-called masses enthusiastically supported the declarations of war and happily boarded the freight-cars rolling to the Western front. But could it be that historians merely copied this view from each other without scrutinising the evidence? One of the first to put a big question mark behind received views of universal nationalistic fervour among the masses was the French historian Jean-Jacques Becker.[10] Having unearthed the relevant sources for a number of regions in France, he found that there were tears and consternation, rather than mad flag-waving.

On the German side, Fischer was the first to draw attention to the fact that *peace* demonstrations occurred in various cities after the publication of the Austro-Hungarian ultimatum to Serbia.[11] The protesters evidently wanted to warn Vienna not to start a war in the Balkans. The demonstrations so worried the German authorities that they thought they would have to respond. The reaction of the military was predictably hardline: they proposed to arrest the ring-leaders and to put the mass of demonstrators under military discipline. Bethmann Hollweg and his civilian advisers were horrified by the proposals of the 'red-baiters in uniform', as Riezler called them. Clearly it would have been disastrous to have a civil war on your hands when you were beginning to prepare for the possibility of a major foreign war. The generals, therefore, were persuaded to desist while the government initiated negotiations with the leadership of the Social Democratic party in the hope of gaining their support for a *defensive* war against Russia. In this they succeeded. As Müller recorded in his diary on 1 August, the day the German mobilisation order was issued: 'The government has succeeded very well in making us appear as the attacked.'

Fischer, in dealing with this dramatic story, was of course primarily interested in its political aspects. But later the historian Volker Ullrich investigated further local reactions to the threat of war towards the end of July 1914 and to the proclamation of war at the beginning of August.[12] Using sources from the city state of Hamburg, he found that the *Hamburgische Correspondent,* a respectable middle-class paper, reported that the news of the mobilisation had been received 'in silent earnestness'. Ullrich, moreover, found the diary of a member of the socialist Youth League which contains the following passage: 'Excitement among the population which expressed itself in a panicky run on savings banks and grocery shops. Most people were downcast, as if they were to be beheaded on the following day.' And finally there is the response of an older Social Democrat in Hamburg who wrote on the day the Reichstag voted the war credits: 'In front of the trade union offices in Besenbinderhof many comrades assembled day after day. We watched the commotion rather dumbfounded. Many asked themselves: "Am I mad or is it the others?"'

Accessible Sources for Student Researchers

To this day we know astonishingly little about actual popular reactions to the July Crisis and the outbreak of war in other cities or regions of Europe. If the work by Becker and Ullrich provides any guide, a large field is still waiting to be explored here, and it may be worth your while to see whether there is any material in your locality which sheds light on this question. Newspapers should be accessible. But what about unpublished sources? To be sure, it is not suggested here that we shall totally have to revise our views on popular moods in July and August 1914. However, it may well turn out, when all the work has been done, that enthusiasm was not as widespread as has been assumed up to now. Most probably there were men and women in other parts of Germany, France, Britain or Austria who were also downcast or who asked themselves whether their fellow-citizens had lost their minds. A third group of people may merely have been pulled along by the cheerleaders in the crowds that were milling through the streets and squares when war was declared.

The time has therefore come to shift our perspective. For the past 65 years or so historians of the origins of the First World War have been primarily concerned with high politics and diplomacy. No document in the ministerial files has been left unturned and no tit-bit of information about individual decision-makers at the top has been ignored. No doubt we shall have to go on studying the politics of pre-1914 Europe. But maybe it is time for these themes to be supplemented by questions which the social historians would ask and which would enable us to learn much more about popular moods and mentalities on the eve of the Great War - that catastrophe from which Europe never really recovered.

Notes

1 Z. Steiner, *Britain and the Origins of the First World War*, London, 1977; V.R. Berghahn, *Germany and the Approach of War in 1914*, London, 1973; R. Bosworth, *Italy and the Approach of the First World War*, London, 1983; D. Lieven, *Russia and the Origins of the First World War*, London, 1984; J.F.V. Keiger, *France and the Origins of the First World War*, London, 1983.
2 J. Joll, *The Origins of the First World War*, London, 1984.
3 F. Fischer's second book is the most detailed here: *War of Illusions*, London, 1975.
4 L.F.C. Turner, *Origins of the First World War*, New York, 1967.
5 F. Fischer, *Germany's War Aims in the First World War*, London, 1967.
6 See note 3.
7 For details of the following see V.R. Berghahn, *Germany and the Approach of War in 1914*, London, 1973, pp. 145ff.
8 See, for example, K. Jarausch, *The Enigmatic Chancellor*, New Haven, 1972, pp. 148ff.
9 K.D. Erdmann, ed., *Kurt Riezler - Tagebücher, Aufsätze, Dokumente*, Göttingen, 1972.
10 J.-J. Becker, *1914: Comment les Français sont entrés dans la guerre*, Paris, 1977.
11 For details see F. Fischer, *War of Illusions*, London, 1975, pp. 698ff.
12 V. Ullrich, 'Die Verkündigung des Kriegszustandes' in *Hamburg Rundschau*, 2 August 1984, p. 10.

Questions to consider

• **What are the arguments for a) a 1912 preplanned power-political expansionist war; b) a war as an answer to domestic political difficulties; c) a changing-military-balance preventive war?**

• **What is the evidence, from the sequence of events after the Serajevo assassinations, that the outbreak of a general European war in 1914 came from hastily prepared German plans for a local Balkan confrontation?**

• **Does the Capelle memorandum of the Kaiser's views on 6 July strengthen or weaken the arguments that Germany planned for a major European war to be fought at some time in order to fulfil expansionist power-political aims?**

Further reading: L. Albertini, *The Origins of the War of 1914*, London, 1958. V.R. Berghahn, *Germany and the Approach of War in 1914*, London, 1973. R. Bosworth, *Italy and the Approach of the First World War*, London, 1983. F. Fisher, *War of Illusions*, London, 1975. J. Joll, *The Origins of the First World War*, London, 1984. E. Leed, *No Man's Land*, Cambridge, 1979. A. Marwick, *The Deluge*, London, 1966. J.A. Moser, *The Politics of Illusion*, London, 1975. L.F.C. Turner, *The Origins of the First World War*, London, 1970. B. Waites, *A Class Society at War. England 1914-1918*, Leamington Spa, 1987.

Volker Berghahn, latterly of the University of Warwick and currently Professor of Modern History, Brown University, Rhode Island, USA, is the author of **Germany and the Approach of War in 1914, Macmillan, 1973.**

4 The Rise and Fall of Weimar

Summary: Weimar democracy, which arose from defeat and which replaced a semi-authoritarian imperialist regime, never had very wide support. Despite opposition from right and left the Weimar Republic survived to years of greater internal peace from the mid-1920s, when the fundamental political problems were masked, until exposure by the economic and political crises of 1929.

HITLER'S APPOINTMENT as German chancellor in 1933 was arguably the most important event of the twentieth century. Within six years it led to the vast destruction and profound, world-wide changes of the Second World War. It is therefore crucial for historians to explain so violent, barbaric and destructive a movement came to control an advanced and civilised country. The most direct causes for the collapse of the first German democracy must be sought in the years between the end of the First World War and the establishment of the Third Reich. This period can be divided into three sections: 1918-1924, when the Weimar Republic was set up and survived a series of severe crises; 1924-1929, when the republic was relatively stable and prosperous; and 1929-1933, when renewed instability eventually put an end to democracy with the appointment of Hitler as Reich Chancellor on 30 January 1933.

1918-24: Defeat and New Order Survival

The defeat of 1918 hit the German public with brutal suddenness. To the very end they had been told that victory was within their grasp. In the spring of 1918 the German High Command still staked all on an offensive to achieve the breakthrough on the Western Front which had eluded them since 1914. An all-out victory would perpetuate the semi-authoritarian imperial regime and the privileges of its dominant classes. In fact German resources were by 1918 hopelessly over-stretched and morale at home and in the army had become fragile. At the end of September 1918 the High Command had to acknowledge defeat by asking for an armistice. This precipitated the revolution and the overthrow of the monarchy.

The parliamentary democracy which was established in Germany in 1918/19 was therefore the consequence of defeat and revolution and not the deliberate choice of a majority of the population. They hoped, however, that the removal of the Kaiser and the adoption of parliamentary democracy would make the Allies grant Germany a lenient peace. When the terms of the treaty of Versailles became public in May 1919 many who had briefly supported democracy turned against it. Others, mostly the middle classes previously loyal to the Empire, had never wanted democracy and deeply resented the overthrow of the monarchy. They persuaded themselves that the German army had never been defeated on the battlefield, but had been undermined by subversion on the home front. The men swept to power in the revolution of November 1918 were held responsible for the collapse of civilian morale and accused of betraying the Fatherland for their own ends. This was the notorious 'stab-in-the-back myth'. Democracy and the Weimar Republic were therefore never universally accepted and suffered from a lack of legitimacy. In fair weather a majority might go along with it, but in a time of hardship, as in the Great Depression after 1929, they would desert it.

Why Weimar's Failure was Not Inevitable

Weimar's failure was, however, not inevitable, for the republic survived a period of severe political and economic crisis in its early years. The first threat came from the left, disappointed with the results of the revolution. They wanted a thorough-going transformation of society, as in Russia, based on the workers' and soldiers' councils which had spontaneously sprung up during the German revolution. Such a system had little chance

Troops assemble at the Brandenburg Gate during the Kapp Putsch, 1920

Why Weimar's Failure was Not Inevitable

of being realised in an advanced industrial country like Germany, where, unlike Russia, the workers had long had the vote. The first elections after the fall of the monarchy did not produce a socialist majority and the SPD (Social Democratic Prty of Germany) had to govern in coalition with middle-class parties. Some historians have blamed the Social Democrats led by Friedrich Ebert for being too obsessed with the threat from the left and too reliant on the old imperial officials, particularly the officer corps and the general staff. Without their help, however, Ebert and his colleagues could not have fed the population, maintained law and order and safeguarded the unity of the Reich in 1918/19.

The treaty of Versailles was regarded in Germany as humiliating and incapable of fulfilment. People lost sight of the fact that it left the unified Germany created in 1870 basically intact and in the long run in a strategically strong position, with weak neighbours on its east. Following Versailles, disillusionment with democracy led, in March 1920, to the first attempt by right-wing nationalists to overthrow the republic, the Kapp Putsch. At this point pro-republican forces, the parties of the centre and the left, were still strong enough to frustrate the coup. A general strike played a key role in defeating the plotters.

In the next few years instability was aggravated by accelerating inflation. The German currency had already lost much of its value during the war and Weimar governments were too weak to bring inflation under control. The reparations which Germany was obliged to pay under the peace settlement, and which were the subject of international negotiations from 1920 onwards, gave the Reich governments no incentive to put their finances in order. Moreover, by letting inflation continue, the Germans managed for a time to avoid the post-war slump that hit the other major industrial countries, Britain and America. The French Government under Poincaré felt that Germany was deliberately evading reparations and in January 1923 occupied the Ruhr as a 'productive pledge'. In France the Versailles treaty was regarded as having insufficiently safeguarded her security against German aggression and reparations provided a lever through which the French hoped to retain some control over Germany. The economic separation of the Ruhr from the Reich knocked the bottom out of the German currency. By the summer of 1923 there was hyper-inflation; wages had to be paid with washing-baskets full of banknotes and the value of the mark fell hourly. Economic life was in chaos. It looked as if Germany was about to experience the disintegration she had avoided in 1918. In Central Germany there was an attempted Communist uprising; in Bavaria right-wing extremists, led by Adolf Hitler and his National Socialist party, tried to seize power.

The Nazis were one of many extreme right-wing groups whose hallmark was strident nationalism, based on the belief that Germans were an Aryan race, superior particularly to the Slav peoples of Eastern Europe. Most such groups were strongly anti-Semitic, believing that Jews were an alien race within, conspiring against the German people through ideologies such as liberalism and socialism, while as promoters of international capitalism they were undermining the economy of the country. In the social crisis of the post-war period sections of the lower middle class, squeezed between big business and labour and stripped of their savings by inflation, were attracted by National Socialism, simultaneously nationalist, anti-capitalist and anti-Bolshevik. There were similar Fascist movements in other European countries, built around a leader who would impose order and authority. Hitler's movement obtained local prominence in Bavaria through his ability to give violent expression to the resentments and hatreds of people whose security had been shattered by defeat and revolution. In Bavaria the authorities dealt leniently with right-wing violence, for groups such as the Nazis might be needed against another uprising from the extreme left. Thus Hitler and his movement grew, especially in the turmoil of 1923. He was, however, not important enough to control events and in November 1923 the Beer Hall Putsch failed ignominiously.

1924-9: More Stability, Peace and Prosperity but Fundamental Weaknesses Remain

At this point the situation in Germany was changing radically for the better. Not only had all attempts to overthrow the republic from left or right failed, the introduction of a stable currency began the process of economic recovery. A settlement of the reparations problem, the Dawes Plan, was negotiated in 1924. The French occupation of the Ruhr was ended in 1925 and the Locarno Treaty created a greater sense of security in Europe. Germany's western borders were declared final, while her eastern borders could only be changed by agreement, not force. The German representative in these negotiations was Gustav Stresemann, chancellor for three crucial months in 1923 and then foreign minister until his death in October 1929, but he was always under virulent attack from the nationalist opposition.

The middle 1920s have often been called the golden years of Weimar. Germany regained something like her pre-war standard of living. The arts flourished, with names that are still famous today, Brecht, Kurt Weill, the *Threepenny Opera*, the Bauhaus. The real strength of the German recovery is, however, still a matter of debate, for political and economic weaknesses continued. It was difficult under the Weimar political system to produce stable government. This is often attributed to the large number of political parties and the need to form coalitions which proved short-lived. The blame for this is put on the electoral system of strict proportional representation, which allowed even small parties to get a few members elected and immediately reflected, without any barrier, the rise and fall of parties. It would not, however, have been possible to introduce in Germany a first-past-the-post electoral system leading to a two-party system along British lines. Five or six major parties had survived from the imperial period and coalition government was unavoidable. Part of the problem was that the parties found it difficult to co-operate. This in turn was aggravated by the existence of extremist parties on the right and the left. It was difficult for the SPD, usually the largest party, to enter into coalition with the middle-class parties, for its working-class voters might then defect to the Communist party, which always had at least a quarter of the left-wing vote. The irreconcilable division of the left was one of the reasons why the Nazis eventually took over with such ease.

The strength of the German economy in the mid-1920s is also still in dispute. It was very dependent on the in-flow of foreign, mainly American capital. The republic tried to meet aspirations for social welfare, for example through the introduction of comprehensive unemployment insurance in 1927. The employers complained that industry was in consequence burdened by heavy social costs and rendered uncompetitive. People who had lost their savings in the great inflation could not be effectively compensated and remained resentful. By 1927 agricultural prices started to fall internationally and German farmers were hard-pressed. Nevertheless, the democratic regime seemed firmly established by 1928. In the Reichstag elections of that year the SPD, the party most closely linked with Weimar, polled nearly 30 per cent of the vote. In contrast the Nazi party, for the first time contesting a national election on its own, obtained only 2.6 per cent and 12 seats out of 491. There was, however, a fragmentation of parties in the centre ground of politics and this facilitated the Nazi breakthrough when crisis struck again.

1929-33: Reduced Support for Centre Parties

The onset of the final crisis of the Weimar Republic is often linked to the Wall Street crash of October 1929, marking the beginning of a world-wide slump of unprecedented severity. In fact the German economy had already shown signs of sluggishness earlier in 1929. Political repercussions in Germany arose in the first place because higher levels of unemployment made the recently established national insurance scheme insolvent. The parties could not agree how to meet the deficit, the right refusing to sanction higher taxes, the left unwilling to see the burden on the workers and the unemployed rise. In March 1930 the broad coalition headed by the SPD fell apart. The new chancellor, Heinrich Brüning, was given the right to use the president's emergency powers under article 48 of the Weimar Constitution to issue decrees. The Reichstag was thus by-passed and was only left with the option of voting Brüning's decrees down. When it did so in July 1930, the president, Hindenburg, sanctioned the dissolution of the Reichstag. Elections had therefore to be held in September 1930, when the Nazi party received eight times as many votes as previously. It became the second-largest party, with 18.3 per cent of the vote and 107 out of 577 deputies.

A great deal of research has gone into explaining the electoral upsurge of the Nazi movement, which by the summer of 1932 had reached a peak of 37.3 per cent of the vote and 230 out of 608 Reichstag deputies, making it much the largest party. In the past historians have emphasised the irrational nature of this explosion, stressing the ruthlessness of Nazi propaganda, the appeal of Hitler's mass meetings, all signs of profound social-psychological disturbance. Recent electoral analyses have shown that the Nazis made their biggest gains among the Protestant middle class. Roman Catholic voters normally attached to the two Catholic parties retained their previous loyalties. The working-class voters of the two left-wing parties, the Social Democrats and the Communists, also proved relatively immune to the Nazi appeal. From this it can be argued that the various middle-class parties, already fragmented in 1928, were no longer seen as capable of protecting the interests of their voters. The Nazis, on the other hand, appealed effectively to the most diverse groups, including a large number of working-class voters not living in big industrial cities and not normally attached to the two left-wing parties. The Nazis claimed to be a movement, not a party, capable of ending the divisiveness of party and class. Before the incompatibility of their offers to different sections became obvious they had acquired total power.

Economic Crisis: Political Misjudgement

The steep decline of the German economy after 1929 was an essential pre-condition for the success of the Nazis, though not in itself a sufficient explanation. Historians still debate whether the German governments of the time, particularly that of Brüning, could have pursued different policies to mitigate the slump. The policies pursued were deflationary, namely the government itself was constantly cutting expenditure to balance its declining revenue, thus adding to the downward pressures in the economy. The alternative would have been to pump money into the economy, the policies that came later to be associated with the British economist John Maynard Keynes. Credit creation would in practice have been difficult. Till the summer of 1931 the slump did not seem to be of exceptional severity. Nobody wanted to slide back into the devastating inflation experienced only a few years earlier and largely caused by the unrestrained printing of money. The reflationary measures hesitatingly adopted in 1932 did not become effective until Hitler was in power and then benefited him.

In the final stages of the crisis the key decisions lay with the president Hindenburg, aged 85, and his advisers. Among them the most important was General Kurt von Schleicher, who represented the Army. Confronted with the apparently irrestibly rising Nazi tide, these men felt that Hitler would have to be brought into government, but without handing him the unlimited power he was demanding. Important interest groups, such as the major industrialists and the big landowners, wanted a stable government, which could not be established without the Nazis. Hitler was, however, not merely the puppet of big business, a Marxist argument not now generally accepted. In May 1932 Hindenburg dropped Brüning and was persuaded by Schleicher to appoint Papen as chancellor. The latter had virtually no support, was unable to strike a deal with Hitler and only survived by repeated dissolutions of the Reichstag. In the second of the resulting elections, in November 1932, the Nazis suffered a severe electoral setback, their vote dropping by over two million or 4 per cent. This lends weight to the argument that Hitler could have been kept out of power. Schleicher himself took office as chancellor in December 1932, but, with the Nazis still the largest party, could not find a stable basis for his government. Papen, originally his creature, felt aggrieved at being displaced, and by late January 1933 had persuaded Hindenburg that he could make the deal with Hitler that would at last bring the Nazi leader 'tamed' into the government. The Hitler cabinet formed on 30 January 1933 contained only two Nazis besides Hitler and it looked as if Papen, supported by other conservative non-Nazis, was the dominant figure. This swiftly proved an illusion. With the levers of power in his hands, and with a massive popular and in part revolutionary movement behind him, Hitler quickly demolished all restraints on his total control. He had achieved a revolution under a cloak of legality.

Hitler did not seize power, but was given it by a back-stairs intrigue. If so many German voters had not supported him he would never have been in the running. Even then it was not inevitable that he should become chancellor, but few fully realised how catastrophic this would prove.

Notes on German parties and their ideologies
Social Democracy, Communism and Marxism. In Germany the Social Democratic Party (SPD) had become the largest party before 1914. While still talking the revolutionary language of Marx, it had in fact become a party committed to reform. Its leaders were catapulted into power in 1918 by revolutionary events not of their making. The left wing of the German socialist movement eventually became consolidated into the Communist Party (KPD), the leaders of which by the early 1920s followed the policy lines laid down from Moscow. While the SPD was the party most fully associated with the establishment and maintenance of the democratic republic, the KPD was strongly anti-republican. In the final years of Weimar the KPD concentrated most of its fire on the SPD, believing that even if this helped to bring Hitler to power his rule would be brief and end in the inevitable overthrow of capitalism predicted by Marx. People on the right-wing of German politics nevertheless tended to lump SPD and KPD together as Marxists.

National Socialism, Fascism and Conservative Nationalism. The National Socialist Workers' Party (NSDAP), Nazis for short, has sometimes been called the German Fascist party. It had many things in common with Fascism in other countries because the personality of Mussolini, influenced Hitler in his early days. National Socialism became, however, much more important and more radical than other varieties of Fascism, so that the general label 'Fascist' hardly describes it adequately. It must also be distinguished from the traditional and conservative forms of German nationalism, though most German conservative nationalists tended to support Nazism and Hitler once they were in power and successful. As opposed to conservative nationalism, National Socialism was a revolutionary and totalitarian doctrine.

Questions to consider

• **Why were the left and right, rather than the parties in the centre, relatively stronger in Germany?**

• **How important was the Army in the Nazi achievement of power?**

• **How important were policies, rather than Hitler's personality or the circumstances, for the extent of support for the Nazis 1929-33?**

Further reading: E.J. Feuchtwanger, *From Weimar to Hitler. Germany 1918-33* (2nd edn., 1995). J. Hiden, *Germany and Europe 1919-1939* (2nd edn., 1993). I. Kershaw, (ed.) *Weimar: Why did German democracy fail?* (1990) I. Kershaw, *Hitler* (1991). A.J. Nicholls, *Weimar and the Rise of Hitler* (3rd edn., 1991). J. Noakes and G. Pridham, (eds.) *Nazism, 1919-1945. A Documentary Reader. Vol. I: The Rise to Power* (1983). D.J.K. Peukert, *The Weimar Republic. The Crisis of Classical Modernity* (1992).

Dr Edgar Feuchtwanger teaches German history and British political history, mostly of the Victorian period, at the University of Southampton. His publications, besides his recent book on the Weimar Republic, include, with Richard Bessel, **Social Change and Political Development in Weimar Germany** *(1981). He was born in Munich where, as a child, he lived opposite Hitler's private flat.*

5   The Rise of Nazism

Summary: The Weimar Republic was weak from the outset and experienced mounting rejection at the polls from middle- and working-class Germans alike. The Nazis were the main beneficiaries, but failed to win an outright majority. However, Germany's élites, who were also hostile to the Republic, eventually brokered or tolerated a Nazi takeover as the best practical anti-republican option.

WHEN ADOLF HITLER was appointed Chancellor (Prime Minister) of the Weimar Republic in January 1933 he owed his success to two factors: popular support and the acquiescence of the German élites. The rise of the Nazis from obscurity to government had been extraordinarily rapid, for the NSDAP (National Socialist German Workers' Party) was little more than a decade old when it took power and it had only fought national elections in its own right for the first time in 1928.[1] Furthermore, on the face of it, Hitler hardly seemed suitable leadership material in a country where status mattered. He came from a relatively obscure, Austrian provincial background and although decorated for bravery as a German soldier during the Great War, was eventually demobilised with the humble rank of corporal. How, then, did the National Socialists succeed in becoming the largest party in Parliament by 1932 and why were Hitler and his violent movement at least acceptable by 1933 to the power brokers in German politics?

There was nothing inevitable about the rise of Nazism, but nor was its growth accidental or a quirk of fate. After the abject failure of Hitler's attempt to topple the Republic by force in November 1923 in the so-called Munich Putsch he resolved to seek a democratic mandate for the destruction of democracy and discovered that German politics provided fertile soil for his ambitions.

A Weak Republic

It had, admittedly, seemed otherwise in the immediate aftermath of defeat in the First World War and revolution. The first post-war elections (to a Constituent Assembly) held in January 1919 revealed overwhelming support for republican parties of the moderate left and centre and the largest such party, the SPD (Social Democrats), dominated the governing coalition. The Constituent Assembly delivered up an open and democratic political system, but the Social Democrats left the old pre-war Empire's public institutions and the commanding heights of the economy largely in the hands of the traditional élites. The Socialists, although informed by a Marxist ideology, were reluctant to experiment with the country's administrative system and economy at a time when stabilisation and the negotiation of tolerable peace terms had, in their view, to take priority. However, this fateful decision provoked outrage on the radical left without reconciling the old right - the military commanders, judges, civil servants and captains of heavy industry - to the fall of the Empire and to the peace treaty the Republic was forced to sign at Versailles in June 1919.

The resulting upheavals cannot be described in detail here, but suffice to say that several years of political turmoil, inflation, reparations payments and repeated foreign military intervention left the republican parties with progressively fewer friends. Even the first parliamentary elections of June 1920 saw the republican coalition garner just 43.6 per cent of the vote; a sharp decline from the 72.4 per cent of January 1919. In every subsequent parliamentary election the majority of votes continued to be cast for parties either indifferent or hostile to the very constitutional order within which they operated. The degree of popular antipathy to the constitution found even more dramatic expression following the death of the first President of the Republic, the Social Democrat, Friedrich Ebert, in 1925. His successor was the wartime leader Field Marshal Paul von Hindenburg, who was elected despite - or perhaps because of - his monarchist sympathies.

Middle-class Hostility to Weimar

At first the National Socialists benefited very little from these trends. A wealth of literature has detailed the alienation of Germany's electorate, the middle classes in particular, from the constitutional order, but Hitler's small Nazi party was not their first port of call and nor would anyone have expected such an obscure and inexperienced party to gain mass support. Instead, the middle classes transferred their political preferences right-wards within the existing party structure, switched support to small, special interest parties, or deserted the parliamentary political scene altogether.

With the important proviso that many working-class voters also backed conservative, liberal and denominational parties, one can see evidence of the rightwards trend in (middle-class) voting preferences in the respective fortunes of the left-liberal DDP (German Democratic Party) and the conservative, monarchist DNVP (German National People's Party). The DDP polled 5.6 million votes (18.6 per cent) in 1919, but just 1.9 million (6.3 per cent) in December 1924, while the DNVP saw its vote rise from 3.1

million (10.3 per cent) to 6.2 million (20.5 per cent) between the same elections. The growth of special interest parties and fundamental alienation from the system had become evident by 1928. Fringe parties had polled just 0.4 million votes in 1919 (1.6 per cent), but 2.3 million (7.5 per cent) by December 1924 and 4.3 million (13.9 per cent) in 1928. By then the DNVP's share of the poll had fallen to 14.2 per cent and overall electoral participation stood at 75.6 per cent, having declined steadily from the 83 per cent of 1919. Furthermore, by the late 1920s, German non-Marxist parties themselves were moving rightwards and appointing new leaders whose personal agendas were more decidedly anti-republican and conservative than those of their predecessors.

The Political Legacy of Imperial Germany

The forces underlying this process have now been analysed very thoroughly. Patterns of political behaviour which had originated in the imperial era continued to influence Weimar politics and help to explain why the Republic failed. The imperial constitution had granted limited powers to the Reichstag while emphasising those of the Emperor, his Chancellor and the cabinet to the point where party politicians had found that lobbying on behalf of particular client groups constituted one of the more meaningful forms of political activity. The middle classes of Germany were very heterogeneous in social and cultural terms, including farmers and guild-based craftsmen whose perspectives were often still pre-industrial, yet also a growing army of white-collar employees, technicians, members of the professions and of the business and industrial élites. The

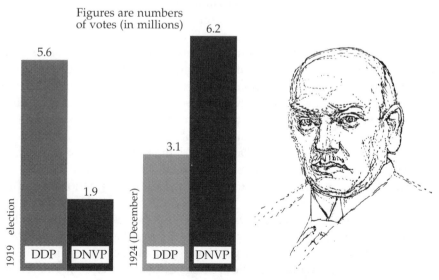

The rightwards trend of middle-class voting, 1919-24 (left), Stresemann (right)

The Political Legacy of Imperial Germany

process of lobbying could address the needs of one, perhaps a couple, of the sectional interests within this diverse social grouping, but precluded the formation of a mass middle-class party, let alone a party which transcended social and cultural barriers altogether.

In Weimar these old habits died hard. The historian Frank Domurad once observed that middle-class support for the centre-right Weimar parties was granted 'in an almost contractual fashion',[2] but the parties themselves found it hard to meet their followers' expectations. For a start the economic and political climate was far less propitious than it had been under the Emperor, leaving fewer spoils to share out, but the nature of political life had also changed. It was one thing to ask favours of an Imperial Chancellor, but quite another to seek advantages for a narrowly-defined social group within an open parliamentary system where other, often conflicting interests predominated. And bourgeois politicians found it particularly alarming that the problem focused not merely on a gaggle of competing middle-class interests, but on the presence of a large labour party, the SPD, which typically commanded a quarter of the vote. If one added to that the 10 per cent of votes for the Communists (KPD) and the 13 per cent of votes for the Catholic Centre Party, which was pro-republican at least until 1929, the problem became all the more acute. Middle-class parties and voters came to mourn the pathological fragmentation of their political life, yet seemed incapable of addressing the problem constructively.

The Growth of Small Special Interest Parties

As noted, small protest parties proliferated, representing even more finely differentiated interests, sometimes regional sometimes economic, than could the conventional parties. Some defended the relatively wealthy, others the victims of past economic disasters such as the great inflation of 1923, and others the farming population which by 1928 was already feeling the effects of the gathering economic storm. Jeremy Noakes remarked that the inability of the DNVP to prevent or solve the mounting agricultural crisis precipitated desertions to extraparliamentary peasant groups such as the Landvolk,[3] while Thomas Childers observes that about a third of middle-class voters had already abandoned their traditional conservative and liberal parties before the onset of the Great Depression in 1929.[4]

The Nazi breakthrough, at state level in 1929 and at national level in 1930 has, therefore, until recently focused specifically on the crisis of the middle classes in Germany. The Depression, so it has been argued, was the catalyst which precipitated a growing tide of desertions to the NSDAP which eventually mobilised a large proportion of the Protestant middle classes in particular. Many Catholics remained loyal to the Centre Party or, in Bavaria, to the BVP (Bavarian People's Party).

Quite apart from this powerful body of circumstantial evidence, the sociology of the Nazis' constituency appeared to lend powerful support to the middle-class hypothesis. The combined vote of the labour parties (SPD and KPD) remained virtually unchanged during the death throes of Weimar, but electoral support for the liberal and conservative parties evaporated as the Nazis' vote surged. Furthermore, membership records, such as they were, pointed to the domination of the NSDAP by its paid-up middle-class membership. When in 1969 Karl-Dietrich Bracher completed his seminal history of National Socialism, *The German Dictatorship*, he therefore subscribed unreservedly to the middle-class hypothesis of Nazism. Workers were, he concluded, conspicuous by their absence.[5] The late Martin Broszat was less adamant,[6] but it was only during the 1980s that new research began to destroy the old certainties.

The NSDAP - a Party for All Germans

Both the membership of the Nazi movement and its electoral support are now perceived as far more heterogeneous in social terms. Two North American historians, Thomas Childers and Richard Hamilton, published key studies of the Nazi electorate which emphasised its social diversity,[7] but the greatest and ultimately decisive revisions to the traditional picture have come from the pen (or computer!) of the German political scientist Jürgen Falter. He demonstrates that the NSDAP did, indeed, have some difficulties in attracting Catholic voters, but in other respects the social profile of the Nazi electorate was extraordinarily diverse and remarkably similar to that of the electorate as a whole in terms of age, gender and class. Looking specifically at the class dimension Falter confirms that an impressive proportion of Protestant middle-class voters did, indeed, turn to the NSDAP, but so did many workers from a wide variety of political traditions and social contexts. So many that by July 1932 more were voting NSDAP than either SPD or KPD.[8]

Work by Detlef Mühlberger and Conan Fischer, among others, has established that the paid-up membership of the Nazi mass organisations, the party and the SA (storm troopers), was similarly diverse in social terms.[9] There was a certain bias towards the middle classes within the party which was offset by a similar bias towards the working classes in the SA. The most pronounced distortions in social profile had nothing to do with class, focusing instead on gender and age. Very few women joined the party with its male-orientated ethos and none, of course, were permitted to join the paramilitary SA.[9] It has always been acknowledged that the Nazi movement was comparatively youthful.

As the strength of working-class support for the Nazis became increasingly apparent, some defenders of the old orthodoxies fought a rearguard action which focused on the alleged nature of the National

Socialists' working-class constituency. These were 'Tory' workers, it was claimed, who had never supported the Marxist parties, or they were from the rural backwaters of Germany, or employed in the public sector. Whatever, they were deemed 'atypical' workers whose perspectives and lifestyles were comparable in many ways with those of the middle classes.

With regard to the Nazi electorate it appears that rural workers were more inclined to vote Nazi than urban workers (with town-dwellers falling in between). However, the distinctions were relatively slight and eclipsed by the impact of religion; Protestant, urban working-class areas delivered up a much higher vote for the NSDAP than did Catholic, rural working-class areas. Similarly, both workers from Marxist and non-Marxist backgrounds switched to the NSDAP during the early 1930s. Turning to party activists one is hard put to find significant numbers of farm workers in either the party or the SA. The typical working-class Nazi was employed in a characteristic branch of the manufacturing or industrial economy. Recent work by Gunther Mai, among others, has reinforced this impression by highlighting the limited but significant success of the Nazis' blue- and white-collar labour union, the NSBO, before and immediately after Hitler's seizure of power.

The Appeal of Nazism

At the end of the day the Nazis had achieved precisely what they set out to do - to create a mass movement which transcended the traditional fault lines in German society and politics. As Adolf Hitler had declared in March 1930:

> It is madness to believe that a single occupational group can exclude itself from the German community which shares in the same fate; it is a crime to set farmers and city dwellers against one another, for they are bound together for better or for worse.

Similarly, he rejected any suggestion that the NSDAP was either 'bourgeois' or 'proletarian'; it was 'German' and sought to unite all Germans in a national ethnic community (*Volksgemeinschaft*) where, despite material inequality and a desire to confine women to the household or appropriate types of work, everyone would be accorded the same moral worth.[10] In the July 1932 elections over 37 per cent of votes were cast for this mass people's party, in March 1933 after Hitler had been appointed Chancellor almost 44 per cent.

How had the Nazis pulled off this political coup? It has already been noted that middle-class Germans were increasingly apprehensive and frustrated by their lack of political clout in Weimar and that many subsequently turned to the Nazis. Until recently it was widely agreed that the NSDAP, therefore, had rallied the middle classes under a single banner so as to resist and even destroy the working-class parties and trade unions. The Nazis' advocacy of a socialism based on common national interests rather than common (working-)class interests and their advocacy of a national ethnic community was accordingly seen as little more than a fig leaf behind which lurked middle-class interests dressed up in fresh rhetoric. However, this explanation is strained beyond reasonable limits by the presence of hundreds of thousands of workers within the Nazi movement and the fact that millions of workers voted Nazi.

This author therefore recently suggested that rather than seeing Nazism as the pursuit of the old politics by new means, it might better be perceived as an escape route from the old politics altogether. Middle-class Nazis, terrified by the spectre of socialism or still worse Bolshevism, evidently perceived National Socialism as a means of short-circuiting the politics of class. But by the same token most working-class Nazis must also have sought the end of the old politics. Those from the political centre or right had never been class warriors in any case. Those from the left reflected that hyperinflation, crippling reparations and then a cataclysmic slump in which tumbling government tax receipts and mass unemployment destroyed the Weimar welfare system were a pretty poor monument to the democratic Marxism of the SPD. In May 1932 the NSDAP's National Organiser, Gregor Strasser, spoke in Parliament of the need to create jobs through deficit spending - something not even the SPD was willing to contemplate.

Hitler Gains from Conspiracy

Hitler had hoped simply to overwhelm Weimar by obtaining an absolute majority in Parliament, but although the NSDAP was indeed the largest party by July 1932, Germany's proportional representation system denied him the triumph that Britain's first-past-the-post system would have delivered. It was at this point that the attitude of the élites was critical to Hitler's prospects. As we saw, the old, conservative élites of the German Empire were left almost intact by the 1918/19 Revolution. They tolerated the Republic reluctantly, if at all, and at the end of the 1920s made a concerted attempt to reform the constitution. Their main objective was to reduce the powers of Parliament (where the hated Social Democrats were strongest) and increase the powers of the Presidency which was in the 'safe' hands of the veteran monarchist, Field Marshal Paul von Hindenburg. Many hoped for the eventual restoration of the monarchy.

However, they were not prepared to break the law to achieve these aims, yet could not gather the massive electoral support needed to amend the constitution legally within Parliament. Before 1933 they succeeded in gravely weakening the Republic's constitution, but were unable to destroy it. Thus Hitler and the NSDAP came to be seen as indispensable, for the

Nazis had the popular support the élites lacked and were also hostile both to the Republic and the SPD. For his part Hitler was unable to win an outright majority in Parliament and was therefore willing, by early 1933, to co-operate with the élites to achieve his objectives.

An unholy marriage of convenience was forged between the Nazis and the conservative 'old guard'; a marriage which turned out almost entirely to Hitler's advantage as he destroyed Weimar's political order and replaced it with the criminal and catastrophic National Socialist dictatorship.

Notes

1 The NSDAP won a handful of seats in 1924 as part of a broader extreme right-wing coalition.
2 F. Domurad, 'The Politics of Corporatism' in R. Bessel & E.J. Feuchtwanger (eds.), *Social Change and Political Development in Weimar Germany*, London, 1981, p. 188.
3 J. Noakes, *The Nazi Party in Lower Saxony*, Oxford, 1971, pp. 118-19.
4 T. Childers, 'The middle classes' in D. Blackbourn & R.J. Evans (eds.), *The German Bourgeoisie*, London, 1991, p. 326.
5 K.D. Bracher, *The German Dictatorship*, London, 1973, p. 145.
6 M. Broszat, *The Hitler State*, London, 1981, ch. 2.
7 R. Hamilton, *Who Voted for Hitler?* Princeton, 1982. T. Childers, *The Nazi Voter*, Chapel Hill, 1983.
8 J. Falter, *Hitler's Wähler*, Munich, 1991 , esp. p. 225.
9 C. Fischer, *Stormtroopers*, London, 1983. D. Mühlberger, *Hitler's Followers*, London, 1991.
10 C. Fischer, *The Rise of the Nazis*, Manchester, 1995, Documents 15 and 20.

Questions to consider

• **Why were working-class voters attracted to Nazism?**

• **Why had voters' support for the NSDAP, so limited in 1923-4, increased so much by 1932?**

• **Why did the élites and the Nazis eventually co-operate to destroy the Republic?**

Further Reading: Karl-Dietrich Bracher, *The German Dictatorship,* London, 1971, 1973; Conan Fischer, *The Rise of the Nazis*, Manchester, 1995; Ian Kershaw, *Hitler*, London, 1991; Eberhard Kolb, *The Weimar Republic*, London, 1988; Anthony J. Nicholls, *Weimar and the Rise of Hitler*, London, 1992.

Dr Conan Fischer, University of Strathclyde, is the author of **Stormtroopers: A Social, Economic and Ideological Analysis,** *George Allen & Unwin, 1983;* **The German Communists and the Rise of Nazism,** *Macmillan, 1991; and* **The Rise of the Nazis,** *Manchester University Press, 1995.*

6 The Determinants of German Foreign Policy 1933-9

Summary: There are constraints on a foreign policy, whatever the ideology of a government. Hitler's policy, working within these constraints, had a good deal in common with the policies of other inter-war German right wingers, but there were differences. These differences included a greater willingness to use force, a racial policy against the Jews and the long-term aim to gain *Lebensraum* [living space] in the East. To begin, 1933-8, Hitler achieved his aims without the use of force. Later, for 18 months during 1938-9, German policy had the distinctive mark of *Hitler's* influence. This is seen, in particular, by his decision to speed demands on, and willingness to use force against, Czechoslovakia - decisions which fitted in with the needs of Germany's economic situation and a shifting major-power military balance.

N O HISTORIAN of the Third Reich would deny that Adolf Hitler exerted massive influence on the direction of German foreign policy between 1933 and 1939. It is abundantly clear that he was no helpless puppet manipulated by sinister industrialists in the interests of monopoly capitalism, as he is still depicted in Communist-approved histories of the period. However, to go to the other extreme - as some Hitler biographers have tended to - and imply that one individual, however complete his mastery of the instruments of foreign policy, was responsible for that policy is to misunderstand the nature of the complex processes out of which a foreign policy emerges and to underestimate the real constraints under which individuals, however talented, must operate.

Constants and Variables of German Foreign Policy

There are constants and variables in every foreign-policy equation. Broadly speaking, geographical location, military strategy, economic potential and historical traditions are the constant determinants imposing limits on the options available to any ruler. Individuals or groups of individuals who bring their ideological stock-in-trade - or their 'unspoken assumptions' about the world - to bear on foreign-policy issues are the variables. Apply this to Germany, a country unified only in 1870-1 and flanked by two Great Powers, one of whom deeply resented the change in the balance of power after the battle of Sedan. From the time of Bismarck onwards Imperial Germany struggled to maintain her semi-hegemonal position in a Europe suspicious of the 'Iron Chancellor'. After France and Russia allied in 1892-4 (with Britain not Germany as their enemy) the Reich lived under the threat of a two-front war with corresponding consequences for German military strategy. Germany was also a land of immense economic power, and therefore military potential, well on the way to the commercial domination of Europe by 1900. The dichotomy between Germany's industrial power and her (virtual) diplomatic isolation after 1908 created stresses and strains which led to the First World War. After 1918 Germany, whose economic potential was not seriously affected by the peace treaties, was no more likely to accept defeat than France had been after 1871. Foreign Office personnel, the diplomatic corps, army leaders, industrialists and most politicians on the right and centre of the political spectrum were in broad agreement on the desirability of re-establishing Germany as the dominant power in Europe. The new balance of power encouraged these aspirations. The United States whose intervention in 1917 had tipped the military scales decisively against Germany had withdrawn politically from the old continent (though her economic interest there remained considerable). Russia, devastated by the strain of participation in the First World War and now racked by civil war, was no longer a serious factor in European diplomacy for a decade at least, whilst in South Eastern and Central Europe a crop of small states, often at loggerheads with each other, had replaced the old bulwark Austria-Hungary.

The Continuity of German Foreign Policy, 1918-39

How this favourable situation was to be exploited led to differences of opinion in the corridors of power in Berlin. While some, such as General von Seeckt, Chief of the *Reichswehr* [army], dreamt of war with France and of a pact with Russia to destroy Poland; Gustav Stresemann, Foreign Minister of the Weimar Republic from 1924 to 1929, relied on a realistic combination of skilful diplomacy (playing off Britain and the United States against France) and economic imperialism (re-establishing Germany in East European markets). Heinrich Bruening, Chancellor from 1930 to 1932, also relied heavily on economic weapons to achieve political objectives; thus the abortive Customs Union with Austria in 1931 combined the concept of *Anschluss* [political union] with an attempt to open up the markets of South-eastern Europe to German penetration. It is, of course, impossible to say whether an economically powerful and rearmed Germany would have been satisfied with anything less than the restoration of the *status quo* of 1914, including radical revision of the Polish frontier. What we know of the views of most Foreign Office personnel and army leaders does suggest, however, that there was a considerable degree of continuity in the foreign policy of Stresemann, Bruning and Hitler - up to 1941 at least.

Hitler's Particular Additions to German Foreign Policy

There were discontinuities as well as continuities. Firstly, by 1938 Hitler was prepared to use force and run mounting risks to attain these objectives - but one should not perhaps overstress this point for the kind of authoritarian regime which seems to have been almost inevitable by the winter of 1932-33 (and need not have been Nazi-dominated) might well have used force as a weapon of diplomatic coercion. Secondly, the Nazi leadership was committed to a revolutionary racial *Weltanschauung* [worldview]. The Nazis spurned the frontiers of 1914 and dreamt of new racial frontiers in the East to provide Germany with *Lebensraum* [living space] at the expense of 'Jewish-Bolshevik' Russia, a state which they intended to destroy to make the world safe for the Aryan race. For economic and geopolitical factors were not decisive in this *Weltanschauung* but a paranoid conviction that World Jewry, which, so they thought, had Soviet Russia in its grip, intended to enslave the whole of mankind. To defend Europe against this 'threat' was Germany's special mission under the Nazis and to that end she must rearm as quickly as possible. The brutal treatment of Poland during the war, the mass deportations and, above all, the murder of six and a half million Jews in the holocaust is proof positive that Hitler and his henchmen took their crazy racism and anti-Semitism seriously.

German foreign policy falls naturally into two periods: 1933-7 and 1938-9. During the first period Hitler acted within the framework imposed on Germany by her military and economic weakness; a country with an army of only 100,000 men and six million unemployed was in no position to play *Grossmachtpolitik* [great power politics]. Speaking to the Nazi Oberbürgermeister of Hamburg in March 1933 Hitler expressly repudiated the chauvinistic sabre-rattling emanating from certain conservative-nationalist quarters; an unarmed Germany would, he thought, have to move cautiously and needed six years of peace and economic upsurge to become strong again.

Low-risk Policies Achieved Without War

In these years Hitler was fortunate in being able to exploit the international situation with a minimum of risk. When he finally decided - under pressure from the military who did not want to be bound by arms-limitation agreements - to leave the Disarmament Conference and the League of Nations he acted in the knowledge that Britain, Italy and the United States sympathised with the German demand for equality with other powers in respect of armaments. This left France isolated and unable to move against Germany. Similarly, in 1935, when he reintroduced conscription, he benefited from the fact that the failure of direct negotiations between the Great Powers in 1934 to limit armaments resigned them to the inevitability of German rearmament. And when he ordered the reoccupation of the demilitarised Rhineland, in March 1936, once again the risks were minimal, despite his dramatisation of the episode, for he guessed correctly - as did Foreign Minister von Neurath - that Britain and France, in dispute with Italy over Abyssinia, would not act against a flagrant breach of the Versailles Treaty. Only over Austria did he act incautiously. Apparently confident that the great powers would regard this small country as a virtual dependency of the Reich, he bullied it incessantly in the hope of bringing the Austrian Nazis to power. But when the murder of Chancellor Dollfuss during the abortive Putsch in July 1934 (of which Hitler may have known nothing in detail but clearly approved in principle) aroused the Great Powers, he quickly back-tracked and placated the Austrians for some years.

Hitler's Long-term Aims Revealed

Of course, while Hitler was posing as a reasonable man who wanted only equality of status for Germany and expressly repudiated war as an instrument of policy, in private he was revealing his continued commitment to the expansionist policy outlined years before in *Mein Kampf.* Addressing a group of army and navy leaders in February 1933 he spoke of 'the conquest of new living space in the east and its ruthless Germanisation'.[1] A year later, speaking to generals, SA and SS leaders, he expressed his belief that an economic recession could only be remedied 'by creating living space for the surplus population'. To obtain this '... short decisive blows to the west and then to the east could be necessary'.[2] From a newly discovered source we learn the war with Russia was very much in his mind in 1936-7; in July 1936 he told his confidant Goebbels that in the event of a Russo-Japanese war 'this colossus will start to totter. And then our great hour will have arrived. Then we must supply ourselves with land for 100 years'; and in February 1937 he spoke of 'a great world show-down' in five or six years, that is, 1942-3.[3]

No doubt Hitler regarded the outbreak of civil war in Spain between 'Reds' and 'Whites', the advent to power of a 'Marxist' (*Front Populaire*) government in France and the ratification of the Franco-Soviet pact as proof that Bolshevism was on the march and that Germany must at all costs accelerate her rearmament.[4] Nevertheless, one must not assume that his obsession with 'Bolshevism' was the only reason for the quickening pace of German policy in 1938-9.

Calculations on the Time to Use Force

At the secret Hossbach Conference held in the Reich Chancellery on

5 November 1937 and attended by the three Commanders-in-Chief, War Minister von Blomberg and Foreign Secretary von Neurath, Hitler emphasised the other determinants of his policy. First came military considerations. Rearmament, greatly accelerated since the introduction of the Four Year Plan in 1936, would not be completed until the mid-1940s. By then Germany would be ready for the major conflict Hitler thought inevitable once Germany made her bid to dominate Europe from the Atlantic to the Urals. 1943-5 would be the deadline for action because as he remarked: 'Our relative strength would decline in relation to the rearmament which would by then have been carried out by the rest of the

Part of Germany

Hitler's plan: expansion in the east

Berlin •

Poland

9

8

2

6

7

1

4

3

5

Territorial Changes 1935-9

1 Saarland to Germany after a plebiscite, 1935
2 Rhineland remilitarised, 1936
3 Austrian *Anschluss*, 1938
4 Sudetenland gained by Germany, 1938
5 Slovak border taken by Hungary, 1938
6 Bohemia-Moravia made a German Protectorate, 1939

7 Slovakia an 'independent' state, 1939
8 Ruthenia taken by Hungary, 1939
9 Memelland taken by Germany, 1939
• Germany invaded Poland, 1 September 1939
• Britain and France declared war on Germany, 3 September 1939

Calculations on the Time to Use Force

world ... the world ... was increasing its counter-measures from year to year ... Nobody knew today what the situation would be in the years 1943-5. One thing was certain, that we could wait no longer'.[5] In other words as Britain, France and Russia began to rearm in the mid-1930s time was beginning to run out for Germany.

Germany's Probable Enemies Made Clear

The international scene confirmed this diagnosis. Hitler's hope of securing a British alliance - described in *Mein Kampf* as an essential condition for German domination of Europe - had vanished by the summer of 1936. Britain and France were now bracketed together as 'hate-inspired antagonists'. Moreover, in October 1937, President Roosevelt made no secret of his loathing for Fascist dictators in the famous 'Quarantine' speech. It was not impossible that in the future Germany with only Italy as an ally (and that not until 1939) would face a triple alliance disposing of immense economic potential and capable of ending German hopes of expansion. On the other hand Britain and France were still relatively weak militarily. And France was tagging along behind Britain whose Prime Minister, Chamberlain, was bent on appeasing the dictators. Therefore, Hitler assumed that for the time being they would not oppose Germany if she seized Austria and Czechoslovakia. German military plans were accordingly modified in December 1937; priority was given to the so-called Plan Green for a surprise attack on Czechoslovakia in time of peace, a decision which signified a shift from a defensive to an offensive strategy. Minimal though Hitler thought the danger of a major war would be, nevertheless he was now ready to run calculated risks to achieve his intermediate objectives. What one might term the 'militarisation' of German foreign policy was about to begin; that is the period when Hitler relied on military force rather than on diplomatic methods to achieve his ends.

This phase did not, in fact, begin with Austria. On the contrary, Hitler relied on diplomatic pressure at first. At the meeting with Chancellor Schuschnigg on 12 February he bullied and coaxed the Austrian into agreeing to considerable concessions to the Austrian Nazis which might well have paved the way to a peaceful *Anschluss*. It was Schuschnigg who upset this plan by announcing a plebiscite to allow the Austrians to decide their own future. Again massive pressure was brought to bear on Austria to withdraw the plebiscite and then to replace Schuschnigg as Chancellor by the pro-German Seyss-Inquart. The invasion of Austria only took place when Hitler was absolutely certain that the Austrians would not resist, that the new Austrian government had (at German dictation) formally invited German troops in and that Mussolini would not come to the aid of the Austrians as he had done in 1934.

Hitler's Influence, 1938-9

It is obvious that Hitler played a crucially important role in determining the pace and style of German policy in the 18 months between the beginning of the Czech crisis and the outbreak of war in September 1939. It was Hitler who began the militarisation of German policy when in April 1938 he ordered preparations to be made for an attack on Czechoslovakia in the autumn. It was Hitler who ordered Henlein, the Sudeten German leader, to avoid any settlement of Sudeten German grievances. And when the crisis deepened in September, with German divisions poised round Czechoslovakia waiting for the order to attack, and when war with Britain and France seemed a possibility, it was Hitler who reluctantly settled at the Munich Conference for much less than the total destruction of Czechoslovakia which had been his objective throughout. Counter-factual history has its uses; had Hitler persisted, and had a major war occurred in September 1938, the outcome might well have been different - Britain without the Spitfires she had in the summer of 1940 might well have been defeated. At the very end of his life Hitler certainly thought he erred in not going to war in 1938. Again it was Hitler who planned the march into Prague in March 1939 and the attack on Poland, and who resolutely avoided any negotiation over Danzig and the Corridor in the summer of 1939.

German troops triumphantly enter Vienna, 1938

Hitler and Common German Interests

Nevertheless, Hitler's actions must be anchored in their proper historical setting. Up to 1941 at least, the desire of Foreign Office, Wehrmacht and the great industrial combines to see Germany become the dominant power in Europe coincided with the territorial ambitions of the Nazi leadership. Much was made in the past - especially by German generals - of the opposition to Hitler during the Czech crisis. Certainly General Beck, Chief of the Army General Staff, was critical of the impending attack, and tried to stir up resistance to it. But recent research reveals that this was in no sense motivated by ethical objections to aggression.[6] On the contrary, Beck considered Czechoslovakia an 'intolerable' neighbour which would have to be eliminated by force. His worry in the main was that Hitler, by premature action before German rearmament was completed, would precipitate a major war which Germany could not win. Significantly, his fears were discounted by most colleagues who believed they could easily defeat Czechoslovakia in 11 days and switch their forces westwards in the unlikely event of western intervention. In short, whatever fears there may have been in some quarters about the consequences of attacking Czechoslovakia prematurely, there was fairly general agreement about the objective.

Nor can one attribute the acceleration in the pace of German foreign policy in 1938-9 simply and solely to what Joachim Fest has called 'a neurasthenic craving for sheer movement' on Hitler's part.[7] Other policy determinants were at least as important as his egocentric belief that he alone could solve Germany's 'problems'.

Economic Influences on German Foreign Policy in the late 1930s

It is sometimes suggested in this connection that Germany's economic difficulties were a major factor impelling Hitler to war. Certainly the overburdened economy was showing typical signs of 'over-heating' by 1938-9; shortages of raw materials and skilled labour were slowing down the pace of rearmament. Hitler was aware of this. He may even have realised, however imperfectly, that it would not be possible to maintain a large army indefinitely, once rearmament was complete. There were hints in the Hossbach Protocol that the alternative to mounting inflation and a possible food crisis (through lack of foreign exchange to pay for imports) was to create a fresh demand for armaments by going to war.[8] And on 22 August 1939, addressing commanding generals before the attack on Poland, he declared bluntly that 'we can hold out in the present economic situation and with all our resources under strain for perhaps 10 to 15 years, but no longer'.[9] But one should not attach too much importance to isolated comments, especially when we know that Hitler was in the habit of using any argument that occurred to him when seeking to convince an audience of the correctness of his decisions. Furthermore, there is no hard evidence that the Nazi leadership had any awareness of a general crisis in the system in 1939. Puzzled and concerned the Nazis may have been by the economic problems they faced. But state control of wages and prices was holding back inflationary pressures and the growing power of SS and Gestapo ensured that signs of overt discontent could be quickly suppressed. Whatever the situation might have been like in a year or two, one cannot say that the economic situation was a major cause of war in 1939. Rather it was a secondary factor which confirmed Hitler in his decision to go to war for quite different reasons. The same is probably true of Hitler's preoccupation with his health at this time; more than once he referred to the likelihood of an early death and the uniqueness of his own position as the executant of German policy. It is impossible to quantify such anxieties but, again, they were probably only a secondary factor confirming him in his decision to go to war.

Military Balance Changes Threaten to Disadvantage Germany

More important than either of these factors was the plain truth that the military balance was beginning to move more quickly than anticipated against Germany. Of course, in his more optimistic moments Hitler still hoped to postpone a major war with Britain (and the United States) until the mid-1940s as his order, in October 1938, for a five-fold increase in the Luftwaffe and his approval, in January 1939, of the Z Plan for a huge navy clearly indicate. At the same time he was disturbed by the acceleration in British rearmament after Munich, as measures for building up the Royal Navy and the RAF begun in 1936 came to fruition. In April 1939 Britain took the unprecedented step of introducing peacetime conscription. Already, in February 1939, he told a group of army officers that 'war must be waged soon because of the rearmament of others'.[10] And on 22 August, when he still hoped that Britain and France would remain neutral during the Polish campaign, he told the assembled company of generals: 'There are a number of favourable circumstances [which he had just outlined to them] which may not prevail in three years' time.'[11] That is, the absolute deadline for action was moving in his mind from 1943-5 to 1942.

Events in 1939 Change Hitler's Plans

The deteriorating international scene was the other major determinant explaining Hitler's willingness to risk a major war. British intervention over Czechoslovakia served notice on Hitler that Britain was not likely to allow German expansion to proceed unchecked. The British guarantee to Poland in March 1939 was further proof of this - in fact the Chamberlain government did not intend war but hoped to check Hitler by other means.

Secondly, negotiations between Germany and Poland had ended in failure by March 1939. Originally, Hitler's intention was to neutralise Poland by negotiating a settlement returning Danzig to Germany and giving Germany extra-territorial rights across the Polish corridor in return for a German declaration of disinterestedness in the Ukraine where Poland had territorial ambitions. This was not, as used to be thought, a step on the road to the conquest of European Russia with Poland as an obedient ally; on the contrary, it was an attempt to safeguard Germany's flank in the event of war with the western powers. As army command thought it unwise to engage in hostilities in the west without a Polish-German understanding, an attack on Poland seemed the only way out of the impasse. Popular as war with Poland would be in Germany, it would clearly increase the risk of war with the western powers before Germany was ready for a major war. Thirdly, when Britain and France approached Soviet Russia in the spring of 1939 seeking an understanding to contain Germany, the risk of war on two fronts forced the Germans to take the diplomatic initiative. The outcome was the Russo-German Non-Agression Pact in August 1939. At a stroke the threat of a two-front war was removed and Hitler was encouraged to think that the western powers would not intervene. The attack on Poland, about which Hitler may well have had doubts in the early summer, now became an absolute certainty. When, after all, Britain and France declared war on Germany on 3 September Hitler's calculations were upset and Germany found herself engaged in a major war for which she was not yet ready. This, however, is said with hindsight. Had Germany been able to defeat Britain as well as France in the summer of 1940 this would not have mattered. It was only when Germany failed to do this but then compounded her failure by attacking Soviet Russia in June 1941 and failed to defeat her in the first six months that Germany's fate was really sealed.

Nothing in this article is intended to imply that rulers or ruling groups are the puppets of Fate, driven on by forces beyond their control, like characters in a Thomas Hardy novel, to ultimate destruction. It is clear from the record of any historical situation that men do make decisions, and that their actions have consequences that matter and that are sometimes not those they intend. My purpose has been the more modest one of trying to apply to Hitler's conduct of foreign affairs in the 1930s the well known aphorism of Karl Marx: 'Men make their own history but they do not make it just as they please; they do not make it under circumstances chosen by themselves but under circumstances directly encountered, given and transmitted from the past'.

Notes

1 J. Noakes and G. Pridham, *Documents on Nazism 1919-1945*, London, 1974, p. 509.

2 Robert J. O'Neill, *The German Army and the Nazi Party 1933-1939*, London, 1966, pp. 40-41.

3 Ian Kershaw, *The Nazi Dictatorship. Problems and Perspectives of Interpretation*, London, 1985, p. 123.

4   J. Noakes and G. Pridham, *op. cit.* pp. 401-3.
5   *Ibid* p. 526.
6   K-J. Müller, *Armee, Politik und Gesellschaft in Deutschland 1933-1945*, Paderborn, 1979, pp. 51-100.
7   J. Fest, *Hitler*, London, 1979, p. 574.
8   J. Noakes and G. Pridham, *op. cit.* pp. 526-7. 'On the one there was the great Wehrmacht, and the necessity of maintaining it at its present level, … and on the other, the prospect of a lowering of the standard of living … which left no choice but to act'.
9   *Ibid* p. 563.
10 H. Groscurth, *Tagebücher eines Abwehroffiziers 1938-1940,* Stuttgart, 1970, p. 167.
11 J. Noakes and G. Pridham, *op. cit.* p. 563.

Questions to consider

- Why did the 'militarisation' of German foreign policy begin in 1938?

- Chamberlain's 'appeasement' policy prevented war between Britain and Germany in 1938, a war in which defeat of Britain was more likely than if a war started later. Is a reassessment necessary, therefore, of the appeasement policy in Britain, and Hitler's influence on policy in Germany?

- If Nazi and right-wing German foreign policy coincided so much, what was the nature and extent of *Hitler's* influence?

- What are the reasons, in the light of Professor Carr's analysis, for Britain and Germany to be at war in 1939?

- Which was the greatest influence on the outbreak of war between the great powers in 1939: Hitler or circumstance or 'history'?

Further reading: W. Carr, *Hitler. A Study in Personality and Politics,* London, 1978. W. Carr, *Poland to Pearl Harbor. The Making of the Second World War,* London 1985. G. Weinberg, *The Foreign Policy of Hitler's Germany. Starting World War Two 1937-1939,* Chicago and London, 1980. I. Kershaw, *The Nazi Dictatorship. Problems and Perspectives of Interpretation,* London, 1985, Chapter 6.

William Carr generously wrote this article in 1987, when Emeritus Professor, Sheffield University, to help the first A Level History journal, History Review, *founded that year. Held in great affection by his colleagues and students, readers of Modern German History were saddened to lose a notably illuminating historian by his sudden death in 1991.*

7 Did Hitler Want Total War?

Summary: The future of war as 'total war', in which the civilian population and the economy was a part, was the lesson learned by the Great Powers from the First World War. Hitler accepted this but, unlike the German military leaders who saw civilian and economic preparation as a means of defence, Hitler saw preparations for total war as a path to conquest and expansion and the 1936 Four Year Plan initiated economic preparations. This plan, which was later extended to Germany's conquered territories, had large social and economic consequences, including the reduction in living standards, the mobilisation of women in the workforce and the extension of state control. However good Hitler's preparations, Hitler's plans unravelled when the Four Year Plan economy underperformed and Germany found herself at war with the Great Powers sooner than planned.

ALMOST FIFTY YEARS after war broke out in Europe historians are still finding fresh evidence to answer the question that A.J.P. Taylor asked in 1961: what kind of war did Hitler want? Taylor's own answer was controversial. He claimed that Hitler was interested only in reversing the Versailles Settlement; and he used the evidence of an American economist, Burton Klein, who had been a member of the team sent over by the United States to survey the economic effect of bombing, to show that Germany had armed only to a limited extent before 1939. Taylor argued that it was fair to assume that if Hitler had wanted a great war of conquest he would have armed to the teeth to secure it. Limited rearmament meant limited wars and diplomatic opportunism, a view confirmed by the subsequent success of Germany's 'lightning' victories over Poland, Norway, Holland, Belgium and France.

Historians Disagree on the Extent of Hitler's Ambitions

This view has always been difficult to reconcile with what we now know about German ambitions. Hitler's vision of German power in Europe and an empire in the east went well beyond the mere revision of Versailles. The ideas on world power and living-space for the German race which fill the pages of *Mein Kampf* were not mere fantasies from Hitler's political adolescence, but shaped his whole approach to world affairs, and they recur again and again in his discussions of German strategy in the 1930s and 1940s. Germany had to be prepared for the great clash of nations, the *Völkerringen*. The recent publication of the Goebbels' diaries for the 'missing' period of the 1930s, shows Hitler in 1937 talking of the great conflict to come in six or seven years' time, a conflict that would redraw the map of the world by the early 1950s.[1]

Of course, much of this exaggerated and fantastic plan for German empire was well known before 1939 and was confirmed at the post-war Nuremberg trials. The problem was to know how seriously to take it. Klein's evidence that Hitler's war preparations were much more modest than statesmen had assumed in 1939, and that even during the war Germany enjoyed a 'peace-like' war economy until 1942/3, suggested that there was a clear gap between Hitler's vague ambitions and the reality of German economic and military policy. *Mein Kampf* diplomacy might whip up party enthusiasm at home, but it did not necessarily mean waging total war.

Recent research has called this evidence itself into question. There is a growing consensus among historians that not only did Hitler continue throughout the 1930s to think in terms of a great conflict for world power, but that he gradually transformed the German economy, and the military machine that it supported, to the goal of full-scale, total war. The roots of this strategy are to be found not in *Mein Kampf*, but in the shift in military thinking that occurred in Germany long before Hitler came to power.

Total War - the Lesson of the First World War

Total war was the most important lesson that Germany drew from the First World War. Defeat had been brought about because of a lack of economic preparation and the poor resources available to fight against all the major powers. The 'stab-in-the-back' from the home front in 1918 was seen by the army leadership as a direct product of the hardships that Germany's economic problems placed on ordinary people. In the 1920s the German armed forces - and military thinkers elsewhere as well - developed the view that any future war would be a war of civilian populations and economies as much as a war of armies. 'Modern war', wrote Colonel Georg Thomas, future head of Hitler's military headquarters economic branch, 'is no longer a clash of armies, but a struggle for the existence of the peoples involved'.[2] The only way to prevent German defeat in the future was to prepare in peacetime to mobilise the whole society and economy for war and to create close links between the economic development of the State and its military requirements. The German forces called this concept *Wehrwirtschaft*, the 'defence-based economy'.

Hitler's Differences with German Army Leaders

When Hitler came to power he brought with him his own views on total war. He was obsessed with the lessons of the Great War. He was determined that rearmament would extend into all areas of German economic life. He was caught up in the idea that any future war would be a life or death 'struggle for existence', and that no effort was too great to ensure that in that struggle Germany would prevail. His views coincided closely with those of the military leaders. The real difference was a difference in strategic direction. The armed forces were anxious to create an adequate means of defence for a Germany that had been defenceless since 1919. In 1933 there were wild rumours that Poland was about to attack Germany. Army leaders ruefully noted that in this event, Poland would win. Hitler's aims went much further; he wanted to rearm Germany so that she could continue the path of expansion and imperialism that had been rudely ended by the Great War.

Economic Preparations for a Nation at Arms

In the early stages of German rearmament these differences did not matter. Hitler was not going to place his regime in jeopardy by risking an active foreign policy before the military build-up had really got going, or before Germany had recovered from the damaging effects of the depression and massive unemployment. By 1936 the economy had, to a large extent, recovered, and the party was securely in the political saddle. It was already evident that the western powers would not prevent Hitler from building up German military strength again. All these factors encouraged Hitler to go beyond the limited defensive rearmament of the generals and to begin rearming for German expansion. This shift in strategy required something of a revolution in economic policy. Hitler knew in the summer of 1936 that higher military preparedness could only come if the State extended its control further over the economy, and if Germany became more self-sufficient in the things needed to wage war. This was the background to the establishment on 18 October 1936 of the second Four Year Plan. At its head Hitler placed Hermann Göring, the flamboyant and ruthless architect of the political revolution in 1933 and of the build-up of German air power. Hitler chose him because he was a leader of the movement, was intensely loyal to the Führer, but also had the sort of energy and ruthlessness Hitler knew would be necessary to carry out the rapid transfer of the economy to military tasks. Göring had already made it clear in July 1936 that, in his view, rearmament was *'the* task of German politics'. The Four Year Plan was designed to co-ordinate all the economic preparations for Hitler's great war. Göring himself had no doubt that the Plan was designed to do just that: its scope was to 'determine the whole of

Germany's economic and social policy'. Its ultimate purpose was 'preparing the German economy for total war'.[3]

The 1936 Four Year Plan and its Effects

The Plan had four main priorities: to build up domestic production of materials like oil and synthetic rubber to make Germany free from the threat of blockade; to control German trade so that strategic imports/exports took priority; to retrain the labour force for tasks essential for war; and, finally, to oversee the modernisation of German agriculture so that it could provide the food in case of war. All of these were vital programmes if Germany was ever going to face the prospect of a total war. They were also long-term projects. The oil, rubber and iron-ore programmes did not get going until 1938 and would not be complete before 1944. The expansion of aluminium production for aircraft, or of basic chemicals needed for explosives, began seriously in 1938-9, to be completed by 1943. The effect of all these plans was to bring the State into virtual control of the whole German economy. German leaders called this new system the *gelenkte Wirtschaft*, the managed economy.

The effects of this redirection in German strategy were many. It brought about a political confrontation between the conservatives, who had supported Hitler up to 1936, and the political circles now promoting autarky and large-scale rearmament. The result was the eclipse of the old élite's influence. In 1937 Hjalmar Schacht, the Minister of Economics since 1934 and inspiration behind the economic recovery, was forced to resign; in February 1939 he was sacked outright from the Reichsbank. In early 1938 the conservative foreign minister was removed, the defence minister, General von Blomberg, ousted through a scandal engineered by Göring, and his deputy, General von Fritsch, sacked for allegations of homosexuality. The people who replaced them were all from the Nazi movement; Hitler replaced Blomberg as defence minister and chief of the armed forces; Göring became a self-styled 'economic dictator'; Walther Funk, a notorious homosexual himself, became Economics Minister, and yes-man to Göring; Joachim von Ribbentrop became Foreign Minister, and yes-man to Hitler. By 1938 Hitler had brought the whole German military and economic machine under the direction of himself and his party comrades.

The Four Year Plan and Living Standards

The Four Year Plan also had profound effects on the nature of the German economy. Almost all the extra growth in the economy after 1933 was diverted to the needs of war. Living standards barely returned to the level of 1928, but the economy as a whole had grown 38 per cent by 1938 above the level of 1928 (in real terms). There were wide areas of poverty in the Germany of the 1930s, and by the end of the decade living standards were

The Four Year Plan and Living Standards

beginning to decline. A British businessman visiting Berlin in 1937 noted on his return:

> In the country itself the standard of living seems low compared with ourselves ... The difficulty of the poorer classes obtaining what might be called 'lesser luxuries' i.e. the things just above the level of necessities, is very marked.[4]

Rationing for certain goods was introduced in 1938, and the quality of consumer products declined sharply, as poorer substitute materials replaced traditional imports. State intervention also increased conspicuously. Prices and wages were closely controlled, and offenders given harsh exemplary punishments. Later in the war Hitler was to boast that the cure for inflation 'was to be sought for in our concentration camps'.[5] Industry found itself more and more subject to state controls. The State began to run industries of its own. In 1937 Göring set up the *Reichswerke* 'Hermann Göring' to mine and process Germany's low-grade iron ores. In 1938 and 1939 the *Reichswerke* took over numerous other businesses or founded new ones on greenfield sites. By 1940 it was Europe's largest business, employing 600,000 people. At Salzgitter, in Brunswick, architects began to design a magnificent new industrial city, Hermann-Göring-Stadt, centrepiece of the new Nazified economy.

Extension of the Four Year Plan to Conquered Territories

But despite the great efforts to build up armaments and to create the industrial base for future warfare, it had always been evident to Hitler that the resources of Germany did not match his ambitions. He needed the resources of central and eastern Europe as well. With these under German control, he would be able to build the weapons needed to challenge the Soviet Union, and later to defend Germany's claim to world power status. Between 1938 and 1939 Hitler began to expand directly into central Europe, tearing up the Versailles Treaty as he went, but garnering valuable economic resources to pour into the vast German war effort. Wherever German forces went, the Four Year Plan and the *Reichswerke* were never far behind. In Austria, Czechoslovakia, and later in Poland, the coal, iron-ore, steel production, machinery and armaments industries were integrated immediately with the programmes of the German economy and armed forces, usually by the *Reichswerke*. The first stage of German expansion was to provide the economic springboard for the great wars Hitler was now planning to east and west.

Radical Rearmament from 1938

In late 1938 and early 1939 Hitler laid down the plans to turn Germany into a military super-power by the mid-1940s. Using the resources released for war at home and from the captured areas, he ordered a quintupling of the air force, a vast new battle fleet to challenge western naval power, and army weapons and explosives higher than the peak reached in the First World War. In 1918 Germany produced 196,000 machine guns; in 1939 Hitler ordered two million a year. This was scarcely the armoury for limited war. By 1939 war preparations soaked up 23 per cent of the German national product. If the industrial programmes of the Four Year Plan are added the figure is even higher. Hitler was now embarked on a burst of military expenditure to prepare the superstructure of weapons production on the substructure of industrial resources. This was to be the great war 'by 1943-5',[6] but one in which the mistakes of 1914 would be avoided. There would be no two-front war, and Germany would be prepared to transform her economy instantly, on the outbreak of war, into a massive war machine. Hitler was determined that this time Germany should win.

Total War or Local War in 1939?

Yet even if Hitler did want a great war, historians have argued that the social and economic cost of trying to prepare for it caused the German economy to 'overheat', and that in 1939 Hitler was faced with a serious economic crisis and fear of popular unrest. Because of these domestic pressures, brought about by the nature of his war preparations, Hitler was forced to go to war with the west in 1939. Once again recent research has

A military parade passes 'Unter den Linden', Berlin, in 1936

Total War or Local War in 1939?

questioned these assumptions. There is little evidence of social unrest or political threat in 1939. 'Trust in the Führer and pride in German policy among the population is boundless. Everyone is sympathetic', ran an internal party report in August 1939.[7] Ian Kershaw has recently argued that in 1939 the long run of bloodless victories had created popular support for Hitler much broader than he had in 1933. But, in addition, the security system and the many ways of enforcing allegiance and obedience by 1939 made it almost impossible to protest effectively. Though many Germans did not relish the prospect of war, most were confident, in the summer of 1939, that Hitler's 'genius' would once again secure his prize without war. Nor is there much evidence that Hitler launched a general war in the west in 1939 to avoid economic crisis. For, from Munich onwards, he and his entourage became confident - overconfident - that the war would be localised, and that Britain and France would make protests, but would not seriously fight over Danzig.

This is the central point. Hitler's plans for a great war were extremely programmatic. His preparations for this kind of war were timetabled to be finished during the period 1943-5. A local war with Poland was, of course, another matter; Germany was well prepared to defeat the Poles in 1939. Conquest of Poland would help in these preparations for larger conflict, by securing additional labour, agricultural produce and the coal and steel industry of Polish Silesia. But the Nazi-Soviet Pact in August 1939, the alliance with Italy the previous May, and his information on the military weakness and divisions in the western powers, all helped to underline his conviction that war would be localised. German preparations in the summer of 1939 were much less frantic than in France or Britain. Hitler ordered only partial economic mobilisation for a local war. He called the western powers' bluff, convinced to the end that the result would be political upheaval and loss of face in Britain and France, while he would win a free hand in the east.

A.J.P. Taylor was right to suggest that the origins of the war have to be sought in the changing attitude of Britain and France to the rise of Germany, a change which dated from shortly after Munich and left both powers with little choice but to oppose Hitler by force in September 1939. The German war machine was not yet ready for this fight, though it was more than a match for Poland, and, as it turned out, France too. In the autumn of 1939 most industrial sectors had not even got their full mobilisation plans. There were few long-term stocks of vital materials. The construction projects of the Four Year Plan were still only half-completed. The German military had not even thought seriously about what kind of war to fight, and the naval power and long-range bombers that they needed to get at Britain were still some years away. But Hitler was determined to prosecute the war as if it were still possible to have total mobilisation. On 4 September the 'total living and fighting power of the nation' was committed to war. He told Birger Dahlerus, the Swedish intermediary who had been trying to reach agreement between Britain and Germany in the last days of the Polish crisis, 'If it is necessary, I shall fight for ten years'.[8]

This was an important decision for, although Hitler hoped to defeat the western powers with a great blow in 1940, before turning back to the east, he recognised that the commitment to total war was still necessary. He was not going to risk what the Kaiser had risked - that war would be 'over by Christmas'. The economy was ordered to change over as fully as possible to waging war. When the conflict was over, there would be spoils for all.

The Effects of War within Germany

From the start, the ordinary German did not have an 'easy war'. Unlike Britain, where rationing was only gradually introduced for certain foodstuffs in the first two years of war, Germany introduced comprehensive rationing from the first weeks of the war. Ration coupons were sent out to all Germans, restricting them to an increasingly monotonous diet of vegetables and black rye bread, with small amounts of meat, butter and a single egg per week. Goods which were never rationed in Britain throughout the war were rationed. The rationing extended to all sorts of articles. By 1941 women were allowed only one and a half cigarettes a day; hot water was permitted on only two days a week. Clothes and shoes became virtually unobtainable for many Germans. When a new pair of shoes was needed it had to be exchanged for the old ones. Work shoes could not be worn outside the factory or office where they were issued. Nazi officials made regular checks on 'suspect' households, and any extra shoes, over and above what was really necessary, were confiscated. The result was a cut in *per capita* consumption of 18 per cent by 1941, against only 15 per cent in Britain.[9] Rationing had the great merit that it ensured fair shares for all, Hitler's real aim, but it signalled to Germans from the very start of the war that they would have to make sacrifices for the war effort. A joke circulated in Berlin in the first winter of the war comparing Gandhi and Hitler: 'What is the difference between India and Germany? In India one man starves for all, in Germany all starve for one man!'

Germans did not starve during the war, but the remorseless demands of the armed forces, the ever greater levels of production ordered by Hitler in 1940 and 1941 (an army equal 'to all other enemy armies put together'),[10] made life for ordinary Germans spartan and strenuous. This was particularly true for women. The myth has somehow taken root that Germany's female population did not contribute to the war effort as did the women of Britain or America. In fact the proportion of women in Germany which worked was exceptionally high already in 1939 - 14 million were in the workforce - due partly to the demands of a fully employed, rearming economy, partly to the rapid exodus of male workers from agriculture. More and more women were left to do the work on the farm - a situation portrayed vividly in the recent German film *Heimat*. In 1939, women made up 37 per cent of the labour force, but only 25 per cent in Britain. By 1944 the German figure was 51 per cent, the British 36 per cent.[11] Many women were compelled to work long hours in war industry, and then to queue for rations, or run the household. Doctors all over Germany in 1939 and 1940 were reporting widespread signs of exhaustion and 'nervous depression' among the female population.

Other women in 'consumer' industry found themselves working on war orders for uniforms and military equipment of all kinds. By 1941 almost half the output from these sectors went not to civilians but to the armed forces. Other women were left to run the family farm or shop now that the males were conscripted. While it was possible to return a skilled metalworker back to his job (and his family) to make weapons, no one argued that farmers and shopkeepers should get the same privilege. Women worked long hours, with little help, until more foreign labour was brought in to keep agriculture going in the middle of the war. After that, ordinary Germans had to cope with the bombing, which brought another kind of hardship that social historians are now beginning to examine seriously for the first time. It is against this background, of declining living conditions, monotonous and irregular food supplies and long hours, that the victimisation and brutality displayed towards foreign forced labour can be better understood. Here at last were people who were worse off than ordinary Germans; as the bombing grew more severe and the German armies retreated, there were plenty of Germans who thought it should be kept that way.

How Germany's Economic Plan went Wrong

The underlying irony is that for all the talk of total war and *Wehrwirtschaft*, Germany failed to match the output of economies less well endowed with resources and skilled labour than she was. Germany also failed to exploit the areas she conquered very effectively. It was this failure to produce enough weapons from the continent-wide resources at her disposal that had persuaded researchers like Klein, in the first place, that Germany was not preparing for, or prosecuting, total war. The real problem Germany faced was the premature outbreak of war, and the very great difficulties faced in trying to wage the 'big war' before all the programmes that would back it up were completed. Much of the early part of the war effort was spent dithering between finishing the great projects of the Four Year Plan or switching instead to the mass-production of weapons. The economy ended up being pulled in both directions, with the result that neither was tackled satisfactorily. There was also very great inefficiency and wastefulness in the war economy, brought about by competition between the armed forces, poor central control of the economy, and military demands for excessively high quality weapons. In 1941 Hitler insisted on a streamlining and rationalisation. In two years the productivity of workers in the armaments sector increased almost three-fold. If war had been postponed until 1943-5 as Hitler had hoped, then Germany would have been much better prepared, and would also have had rockets, jet aircraft, inter-continental bombers, perhaps even atomic weapons. Though Britain and France did not know it, declaring war in 1939 prevented Germany from becoming the super-power Hitler wanted. The drive for total war became instead *Blitzkrieg* by default.

Notes

1 E. Frohlich (ed.), *Die Tagebücher von Joseph Goebbels*, 4 vols, Munich, 1987, III, pp. 26, 55.
2 Cited in B.A. Carroll, *Design for Total War*, The Hague, 1968, p. 40.
3 *Bundesarchiv-Militärarchiv*, Wi 1 F 5.412, Göring conference, 16.7.1938, p. 1.
4 Bank of England, file S 89 (2) Germany, letter from R.L. Barclay to M. Norman.
5 H. Trevor-Roper (ed.), *Hitler's Table Talk*, 1941-44, London, 1973, p. 65.
6 This is the date given in the 'Hossbach Memorandum' of 5 Nov. 1937 meeting, in *Documents on German Foreign Policy*, Ser D, 1, pp. 34-5.
7 *Aus deutschen Urkunden*, p. 211, Kreisleiter report, August 1939, Kreis Darmstadt (unpublished document collection in the Imperial War Museum, London).
8 B. Dahlerus, *The Final Attempt*, London, 1948, p. 119.
9 R.J. Overy, 'Mobilisation for Total War in Germany 1939-1941', *English Historical Review*, 1988, pp. 613-39.
10 Imperial War Museum, FD 5447/45, 'Notiz über die Besprechung bei Chef Heeresrüstung 19.7.1940'.
11 The participation ratio for women (the percentage of the female population aged 14-60 in work) was already 52 per cent in Germany in 1939. It reached a peak in Britain during the war of 48 per cent and in the United States 36 per cent.

Questions to consider

- How did Hitler's idea of total war differ from that of the German military leaders in the early 1930s?

- What is the evidence to support the claim that Hitler planned a major war, the 'clash of nations', for the early/mid-1940s?

- What were the major political miscalculations made by Hitler in preparation for total war?

- Does preparation for total war under Hitler make our understanding of the extent of support for Hitler more or less easy?

Further reading: W. Deist, *The Wehrmacht and German Rearmament*, London, 1982. E. Beck, *Under the Bombs: the German Home Front 1942-45*, Kentucky University Press, 1986. R.J. Overy, *Goering: the 'Iron Man'*, London, 1984. M. Steinert, *Hitler's War and the Germans*, Ohio University Press, 1977. B. Englmann, *In Hitler's Germany*, London, 1988. I. Kershaw, *The Hitler Myth*, Oxford, 1987.

Richard Overy, Professor of Modern History, King's College London. His recent publications include War and the Economy in the Third Reich, *Oxford U. P., 1995.*

How Germany's Economic Plan went Wrong

8 The Hossbach Memorandum

Summary: For the history student the Hossbach Memorandum brings into sharp focus three of the main problems raised by any historical document: Is it authentic? (is it what it claims to be?); What does it actually mean? (what is the essential message conveyed?); What light does it shed on the issues and personalities to which it relates? In this article the Hossbach Memorandum is subjected to these three tests.

THERE CAN BE FEW HISTORICAL DOCUMENTS which have raised so much historical controversy as the Hossbach Memorandum. This document purports to be the record of a meeting held by Hitler with the heads of the German armed services, von Fritsch (army), Raeder (navy), Goering (airforce), von Blomberg (the Minister for War) and von Neurath (the Foreign Secretary) on 5 November 1937. It first came to public notice when it was used by the prosecution team at the Nuremberg War Trials as evidence of the Crimes against Peace with which the accused were charged. Among those in the dock were Goering, Raeder and von Neurath. Von Blomberg had died in gaol before being brought to trial. Von Fritsch was killed fighting with the regiment of which he was honorary colonel in 1939 in Poland. The defence challenged the authenticity of the Hossbach Memorandum and claimed that even if genuine it was not a statement of intent but merely an exploration of available possibilities. The arguments raised at Nuremberg have been echoed by historians and in every discussion of Hitler's foreign policy the Hossbach Memorandum continues to occupy a central place.

The History of the Document

Was the document authentic? As the allied armies swept into Germany in May 1945, orders were given by the German government that all important documents relating to the Nazi regime were to be destroyed. Fortunately for historians, those who were responsible for the archives frequently showed more concern for the security of the records committed to their charge than a readiness to carry out the orders of a regime on the point of collapse. When units of the 1st US army reached the Harz mountains the chief archivist of the German foreign ministry revealed to allied officers the

The History of the Document

locations of thousands of documents which were collected and stored at Schloss Marburg in the American zone. Here they were scrutinised by an Anglo-American team headed by Colonel Thomson, senior translator at the British Foreign Office, and W.R. Perkins of the American State Department. Among the documents discovered was the Hossbach Memorandum, named after Colonel Friedrich Hossbach, Hitler's military adjutant, who had recorded the minutes of the critical meeting which had taken place on 5 November 1937. Hossbach's manuscript was placed in a file with miscellaneous other papers and in 1943 a copy was made by a German officer, Colonel Kirchbach, for the department of military history. It was this copy which fell into American hands in 1945. In common with many other documents it was put on to microfilm by an RAF unit, and sent in this form to the State Department on 25 May 1945. A summary of its contents reached the leading American prosecutor, Robert H. Jackson, on 25 June, and a complete photostat taken from the microfilm of the Memorandum arrived at Nuremberg in September. It was this 'copy of a copy' which Jackson cited in his opening address to the Court on 21 November 1945. The original documents (both Hossbach's and Kirchbach's versions) had by this time disappeared, lost in the files, and have never been recovered. The defence claimed that the Memorandum was a forgery, but Jackson had no doubts as to its authenticity, and this was confirmed when Hossbach published his memoirs, *Zwischen Wehrmacht und Hitler* (Between Wehrmacht and Hitler), in 1949 in which he acknowledged his authorship of the Hossbach Memorandum and the substantial accuracy of the text used at Nuremberg. While its authenticity would seem to be well established, two further points need to be made. Hossbach's record of the meeting was not a verbatim transcript of what was said but a summary, based on notes made at the time, which was written up later. Secondly, as the meeting evidently lasted from 4.30 pm to 8.30 pm, Hossbach must have condensed much of what was said. The text runs to six or seven pages.

The Message of the Hossbach Memorandum

Hitler was not a lucid thinker or exponent of his own ideas. Even in Hossbach's edited summary Hitler ranged arbitrarily from one theme to another with frequent digressions and asides. Though he stated categorically that his hearers should regard his exposition, in the event of his death, as his 'last will and testament', it was hardly a precise list of instructions.

The Memorandum began with Hitler's basic ideas 'concerning the opportunity for the development of our position in the field of foreign affairs and its requirements. ... The aim of German policy was to make secure and to preserve the racial community and to enlarge it. It was, therefore, a question of space ...' He went on to consider two alternative strategies, autarky [economic self-sufficiency] and 'increased participation in the world economy', only to dismiss them as impracticable. Similar reasoning is to be found in *Mein Kampf*. Thus, 'The question for Germany was where could she achieve the greatest gain at the lowest cost?'

Hitler then sketched in the international scene as he saw it. 'Germany had to reckon with two hate-inspired antagonists, Britain and France, to whom a German colossus in the centre of Europe was a thorn in the flesh …' He proceeded to assess the strength of these two countries, pointing out first the weaknesses of the British Empire: 'To sum up, it could be stated that with 45 million Britons the position of the Empire, despite its theoretical soundness, could not in the long run be maintained by power politics'. While France was better placed in relation to her empire she was going to be confronted by 'internal political difficulties'. Having surveyed the potential opposition, Hitler reached the conclusion that: 'The German problem could be solved only by the use of force' and he drew deliberate parallels with Frederick the Great's attack on Silesia and Bismarck's wars with Austria and France. 'If the resort to force with its attendant risks is accepted as the basis of the following exposition, then there remains still to be answered the question "When?" and "How?".'

It was at this point that Hitler directed his attention to the immediate prospect and speculated on how Germany should act. He posited three contingencies, the first of which bore little relation to the second two. In the first, Hitler considered the years 1943-5, by which time the balance of power could only have changed to Germany's disadvantage as other countries rearmed. On these grounds he concluded: 'If the Führer was still living, it was his unalterable determination to solve Germany's problem of space by 1943-5 at the latest. The necessity for action before 1943-5 would arise in contingencies 2 and 3'.

Contingency 2 would occur: 'If internal strife in France should develop into such a crisis as to absorb the French army completely and render it incapable of use for war against Germany'. Contingency 3 would occur: 'If France should be so embroiled in war with another State that she could not proceed against Germany'.

The Memorandum went on to consider how Germany should respond to contingencies 3 and 2 (in that order) and made specific reference for the first time to an attack on Czechoslovakia and Austria: 'It would, of course, be necessary to maintain a strong defence on our western frontier due to the prosecution of the attack on the Czechs and Austria. … Even though the populations concerned, especially that of Czechoslovakia, were not sparse, the annexation of Czechoslovakia and Austria would mean an acquisition of foodstuffs for 5-6 million people. … Should contingency 2, the crippling of France by civil war, occur, the situation thus created by the elimination of our most dangerous opponent must be seized upon, whenever it occurs, for the blow against the Czechs'.

Finally, Hitler drew attention to the situation created by the Spanish Civil War. If Italy could be persuaded to remain in control of the Balearics (Majorca and Minorca) this would be intolerable to France and Britain and might lead to a war of France and England against Italy - 'a war in which Spain, should she be entirely in the hands of the Whites, might come out on the side of Italy's enemies'. In this implausible scenario the defeat of Italy was unlikely and

> If Germany made use of this war to settle the Czech and Austrian questions, it was to be assumed that Britain, herself at war with Italy, would decide not to act against Germany. Without British support, no warlike action by France against Germany was to be expected. The time for our attack on the Czechs and Austria must be made dependent on the course of the Anglo-French-Italian war and would not necessarily coincide with the commencement of military operations by these three States. ... This descent upon the Czechs would have to be carried out with 'lightning speed'.

The Memorandum concluded with a brief account of the ensuing discussion in which von Blomberg and von Fritsch, in particular, voiced their fears of a war with England and France. Their objections were evidently brushed aside: 'the Führer repeated his previous statements and said that he was convinced of Britain's non-participation and that consequently he did not believe in military action by France against Germany'.

The Hossbach Memo and German Foreign Policy

What light does the Hossbach Memorandum shed on German foreign policy? Before one can attempt to answer this question the Hossbach Memorandum must be placed into its historical context. By 1937 the German rearmament programme was in full swing. Conscription had been introduced in 1935, the Rhineland remilitarised in 1936 and German units had been sent to aid Franco in the Spanish Civil War. Some historians see in the Hossbach Memorandum a radicalisation of German foreign policy and the point at which Hitler's implicit objective (*Lebensraum*) became explicit. Others, notably A.J.P. Taylor, have argued that the Hossbach meeting was summoned for internal reasons and that it had little consequence. In the first edition of his book, *The Origins of the Second World War*, Taylor stated that 'Hitler's exposition was in large part day-dreaming, unrelated to what followed in real life' and he confirmed this view in 1965 when he declared that the meeting 'had no significance'. It is not even clear why the Hossbach meeting took place. Noakes and Pridham suggested that the origins of the meeting on 5 November were to be found in the rival demands of the German armed services for Germany's limited steel supplies. The proposed cuts and postponements in the navy's building programme provoked a letter from Admiral Raeder to von Blomberg on 25 October 1937 in which Raeder requested 'an immediate decision by the Führer' (Noakes and Pridham, *Nazism 1919-45*, pp. 679-80). It was the need to produce an agreement on the allocation of steel supplies, that caused Hitler to summon his service chiefs together, and he evidently decided to use the occasion to outline his views on Germany's foreign policy objectives. Alan Bullock finds a further hidden purpose: 'Hitler told Goering before the meeting that he meant to "light a fire" under von Blomberg and von Fritsch as he was dissatisfied with the progress of rearmament of the army' (A. Bullock, *Hitler and Stalin*, p. 617).

What were the Consequences of the Memo?

It is no easier to determine the consequences of the Hossbach Memorandum. Unlike British cabinet minutes it was not circulated to ministers for approval and action. It finished up in foreign ministry files and was neither seen nor signed by Hitler himself. Certain significant consequences have, none the less, been attributed to it. It has been argued by Noakes and Pridharn that Germany's war plan to deal with a threat from France and Czechoslovakia (who were linked by a defensive alliance) was given a more aggressive slant by General Jodl in a directive issued on 7 December 1937. It contained this significant passage:

> When Germany has achieved complete preparedness for war in all spheres, then the military conditions will have been created for carrying out an offensive war against Czechoslovakia, so that the solution of the German problem of living space can be carried to a victorious conclusion even if one or another of the Great Powers intervene against us' (Noakes and Pridham, *Nazism 1919-45*, p. 691).

Bullock sees the importance of the meeting 'not in what was decided, but in the fact that Hitler called it when he did, what he said at it, and the conclusions he drew from it' (Bullock, *Hitler and Stalin*, p. 618). It was the opposition voiced by von Blomberg, von Fritsch and von Neurath, in particular to the war envisaged in the Hossbach Memorandum, that moved Hitler to have them replaced by men more in sympathy with his methods and ambitions. This interpretation finds some confirmation in Hossbach's Memoirs, where he says in relation to von Fritsch and von Blomberg:

> They warned emphatically against the war whose political necessity and moral justification they could not recognize and for which the Wehrmacht in their opinion was not prepared. They

appeared not as submissive puppets but as experienced and conscientious political advisers (F. Hossbach, *Zwischen Wehrmacht und Hitler*, p. 194).

It was this opposition, so Bullock argues, that led to their being replaced, along with von Neurath, who had also seen Hitler to express his doubts in January 1938. All three men were replaced by February 1938. In each case other reasons were given. Blomberg was made to resign on the grounds that he had made an unsuitable second marriage, to a girl with a police record, after she had appeared in a pornographic photograph. Von Fritsch was the victim of a conspiracy hatched by Himmler and Goering. Accused of homosexual practices, he was deliberately confused with a cavalry officer with the same name. He was cleared by a military court, but not reinstated. Von Neurath reached the retirement age of 65 in February 1938, and this was used as an excuse to replace him with von Ribbentrop. Hitler himself took over Blomberg's position as head of the armed forces. Keitel (very much the obedient functionary) became his chief of staff. Von Brauchitsch, notorious for his loyalty to Hitler, replaced von Fritsch. Thus the influence of the traditional élites in the army and the foreign ministry was diminished and Hitler was now surrounded by men ready to do his bidding.

One further consequence of the Hossbach Memorandum was the ending of any hopes of the Anglo-German alliance that had been worked for, at least by Hitler, and had been anticipated in the Anglo-German naval agreement of 1935:

> It cannot be coincidental that Raeder heard at the Hossbach meeting on 5 November 1937 a diatribe against Britain as the 'hate-inspired enemy' and that on the very next Naval war games in the summer of 1938 she figured as the main opponent for the first time (J. Hiden and J. Farquharson, *Explaining Hitler's Germany*, p. 119).

Those who see the Hossbach Memorandum as having little importance point out that none of the contingencies postulated by Hitler came to pass; that the *Anschluss* with Austria in March 1938 appears to have owed more to Goering than to Hitler, and was not planned in advance; that Hitler blew hot and cold during the Czech crisis of 1938, at one moment (20 May) deciding 'not to smash Czechoslovakia by military action in the immediate future without provocation' and a week later giving orders to do just that. Finally, there is in the Hossbach Memorandum no reference to the invasions of Poland or Russia, which were central to Hitler's search for *lebensraum*.

What were the Consequences of the Memo?

General and Particular Conclusions Drawn from the Memo

What then can be learned from this investigation? First, and most obviously, the authenticity of any historical document must be established, and this in a world of micro films and photo copies, not to say faxes and E mail, is not always as easy as it may seem. Secondly, there is no substitute for the whole document. Any summary or paraphrase will lose something of the original, whether of tone, nuance or emphasis. Interpretations of the Hossbach Memorandum differ in accordance with the passages which the historian chooses to stress. Finally, any historical document must be scrutinised in its context and in relation to other evidence. While on its own the Hossbach Memorandum could not prove Germany's responsibility for planning the war, as the prosecution found to its cost at Nuremberg, taken with other evidence it helped to establish Hitler's warlike intentions. Similarly, while the changes to Germany's war plans in December 1937, the changes of personnel in the German high command and the foreign ministry in February 1938 and the changes in German naval strategy, also in 1938, may not be directly attributable to the Hossbach Memorandum, they become more explicable in its light. For these reasons it will continue to be a vital historical source in the interpretation of Nazi foreign policy.

Questions to consider

- In which ways are written minutes of a meeting more useful than audio tapes?

- How can an historian assess the reliability of a brief account of a lengthy meeting?

- What makes an historical document important?

- How does a knowledge of German foreign policy, 1933-9, contribute to our understanding of the Hossbach Memorandum?

- Why is it so difficult to assess the significance of the Hossbach Memorandum?

Further Reading: The fullest text of the Hossbach Memorandum is to be found in *Trial of German Major War Criminals*, HMSO, 1946. A more easily accessible version is contained in J. Noakes and G. Pridham, *Nazism 1919-45*, vol. 3, Exeter University Press, 1988. See also A.J.P. Taylor, *The Origins of the Second World War*, Penguin, 1964. G. Martel (ed.), *The Origins of the Second World War Reconsidered*, Unwin Hyman, 1986. E.M. Robertson (ed.), *The Origins of the Second World War*, Macmillan, 1971. A. Tusa and J. Tusa, *The Nuremberg War Trial*, BBC Books, 1995. A. Bullock, *Hitler and Stalin*, HarperCollins, 1991.

W.O. Simpson is the author of **Working with Sources,** *Stanley Thornes, 1988 and* **The Second Reich,** *Cambridge - Topics in History series, 1995.*